RUDOLF STEINER (1861–1925) called his spiritual philosophy 'anthroposophy', meaning 'wisdom of the human being'. As a highly developed seer, he based his work on direct knowledge and perception of spiritual dimensions. He initiated a modern and universal 'science of spirit', accessible to anyone willing to exercise clear and unprejudiced thinking.

From his spiritual investigations Steiner provided suggestions for the renewal of many activities, including education (both general and special), agriculture, medicine, economics, architecture, science, philosophy, religion and the arts. Today there are thousands of schools, clinics, farms and other organizations involved in practical work based on his principles. His many published works feature his research into the spiritual nature of the human being, the evolution of the world and humanity, and methods of personal development. Steiner wrote some 30 books and delivered over 6000 lectures across Europe. In 1924 he founded the General Anthroposophical Society, which today has branches throughout the world.

FROM THE COURSE OF MY LIFE

Autobiographical Fragments

RUDOLF STEINER

Compiled and edited by Walter Kugler

RUDOLF STEINER PRESS

Translated by Johanna Collis

Rudolf Steiner Press
Hillside House, The Square
Forest Row, RH18 5ES

www.rudolfsteinerpress.com

Published by Rudolf Steiner Press 2013

Originally published in German under the title *Selbstzeugnisse,
Autobiographische Dokumente* by Rudolf Steiner Verlag, Dornach, in 2007

© Rudolf Steiner Verlag 2007
This translation © Rudolf Steiner Press 2013

A catalogue record for this book is available from the British Library

ISBN: 978 1 85584 376 9

Cover design by Morgan Creative featuring an oil painting by Joseph
Rolletschek (*c.* 1894)
Typeset by DP Photosetting, Neath, West Glamorgan
Printed and bound by Gutenberg Press Limited, Malta

Contents

Introduction

'Having an understanding for life'
by Walter Kugler

'As I write this description of my life I feel as though I have departed from the earth,' wrote Rudolf Steiner to his wife on 13 December 1923 after explaining to her that he would be serializing his 'memoirs' in the weekly journal *Das Goetheanum*. In the same breath he then continued: 'In the later chapters covering the 1880s and 1890s I think I shall be able to include a good deal concerning spiritual matters; this will supplement what has been described in the books and lectures.' Here is a clear indication of the significance attached by Rudolf Steiner to the project; and it enables every reader of his autobiography *The Course of My Life* to experience his intentions, for example what he meant in Chapter XXII by 'the nature of meditation and its importance for an insight into the spiritual world'. A highly illuminating contemplation about the contrasts between spirit and matter preceded this in the same chapter, leading to the statement, 'To stand thus with one's mind wholly inside this contrast means having an understanding for life,' for 'Where the contrast seems to have been reduced to harmony the lifeless is holding sway—that which is dead. Where there is life, the unharmonized contrast *is active*; and life itself is the continuous overcoming, but also the recreating, of contrasts.'

The autobiographical accounts by Rudolf Steiner presented in the present anthology are similarly intended as a supplement—now to the autobiography itself: *The Course of*

My Life. Depending on the purpose of their formulation they differ considerably in character.

We begin with the lecture given on 4 February 1913 during the first general meeting of the newly founded Anthroposophical Society. This lecture must surely be seen as the most significant addition to Steiner's autobiography. It covers the period between his birth and the year 1893 and was prompted by a number of slanderous utterances being put about by the leadership of the Theosophical Society with the intention of preparing the membership's mood for the exclusion of the German Section together with Rudolf Steiner, its general secretary. Steiner felt it to be 'highly presumptuous' to lay bare his life before his audience in this way, and he began hesitantly, speaking of himself in the third person. But we are soon deeply moved not only by the gravity but also by the wonderful humour of his presentation as we feel ourselves becoming gradually included in the events he describes.

That lecture is followed by the first of two autobiographical fragments which begins with the puzzling statement: 'My birth falls on 25 February 1861. Two days later I was baptized.' And yet the two CVs and also the second autobiographical fragment give the birth date as 27 February 1861. In years gone by much has been thought and written about this difference in the dates given, with some maintaining that 25 and others that 27 February is correct. The fact remains that 27 February 1861 is the date shown on all the relevant documents such as passports, residence permits and character references as well as in letters sent by Rudolf Steiner to various public authorities. Steiner's own final communication in writing, too, his autobiography *The Course of My Life* written down at the end of 1923, gives 27 February as his date of birth: 'I was born at Kraljevec on 27 February 1861.' Apart from one letter sent to him by Frau von Bredow on 25 February 1921 beginning with the words 'Today which is said to be the birth date of your individuality into this incarnation' (see *Beiträge zur Rudolf Steiner Gesamtausgabe, Booklet 49/50*, p. 5), all those close to him expressed their birthday greetings for 27 February. In keeping with this, celebrations of his birthday at the Goetheanum after 1925 always took place on 27 February. It would have been unlikely for anyone at Dornach to celebrate the day of his baptism (as mentioned in the first autobiographical fragment). It can be stated that his own final communication conclusively gives 27 February as his date of birth and that this concurs with all the official documentation. The editorial principle of a 'definitive edition', i.e. a final edition of works authorized by the writer himself, should be applied with regard to the date of Rudolf Steiner's birth.

A further inconsistency arising in various biographical accounts concerns the country of Steiner's birth. It is correct to say that he was born in Hungary but that his nationality was Austrian. The fact that his parents were Austrian determined his nationality. And he remained an Austrian citizen throughout his life because, despite having numerous friends who interceded on his behalf, he was never granted citizenship in Switzerland where state security was deemed to be threatened by 'communist intrigues' and the 'undermining of psychological sanity by means of unscrupulously practised vampirism'. Since huge sums of money would have been needed by anyone intending to disrupt state security, the informant who contacted the Swiss Attorney General also piled on the agony by claiming that 'treasure in the form of gold is being stockpiled on the premises of the building at

Dornach'. (Letter from C.A. Bernoulli to the Office of the Swiss Attorney General dated 13 May 1921, Federal Archive, Berne.)

There is no indication as to why or when the two auto-biographical fragments were written. The type and style of the second suggests the assumption that it was an account for inclusion in an encyclopedia. But there is no concrete evidence for this. The words 'intuitive' and 'intuition' are used with striking frequency in the second fragment ('knowledge of the spiritual world arrived at through direct intuition', 'seeds of a world view of intuition', 'intuitive-spiritual observation methods', 'intuitive world view of spiritual science'). Perhaps this points to a way of experiencing beings in the sense described in a lecture given in London on 15 April 1922: 'Any degree of Intuition allowed them to experience not only images of the spiritual world but also actual spiritual beings.' (In GA 211, or the compilation *Rudolf Steiner Speaks to the British*, Rudolf Steiner Press, London.)

The small collection of items presented here concludes with a passage from a lecture given in Kassel on 10 May 1914, one of the many autobiographical elements, some less obvious and others entirely pragmatic, which come to light in Rudolf Steiner's lectures. Here he begins with the words: 'I know a man who, in his twenty-third or twenty-fourth year, had a kind of vision.' We could let the matter rest there in the assumption that he was speaking about a person he knew very intimately. However, his meaning is made unmistakably clear in a notebook (NB No. 415) containing his preparatory notes for those 1914 lectures in Kassel. 'My vision of 30 years ago / Record thereof in the [newspaper] *Freie Schlesische Presse*. It was an inept way of expressing what lay asleep in the further recesses of the soul.'

And finally we should remind the reader of the many and in some cases very detailed notes made chiefly by Carlo Septimus Picht (1887–1954) which can be regarded as additional supplementary reading to this book.

Walter Kugler

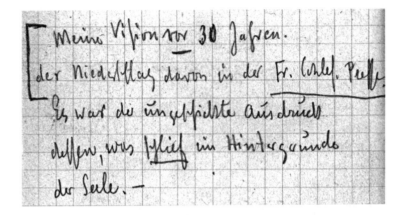

Childhood to Scholarship 1861–93

An autobiographical lecture, Berlin, 4 February 1913

My dear theosophical friends! It is in my honest opinion highly presumptuous to inflict upon a gathering such as this the subject about which I shall be speaking. Since this is how I feel I do beg you to believe me when I say that I only do so because certain aspersions and distortions have recently come to light which it is my duty to gainsay for the sake of our endeavours.

I shall attempt to be as objective as I can in my manner of presentation, while subjectivity shall rule only in the choice of what I consider should be mentioned. Herein I shall be guided principally by what I consider to have had some relevance to my overall spiritual orientation. Please do not regard my manner of presentation as being pretentious in some way but rather as a way of speaking which seems to me to be the most natural.

If someone had chosen to embark upon a thoroughly modern life, a life involving the most modern attainments of the present day, by selecting conditions which would best befit his current incarnation, it seems to me that he would have made the very choices made by Rudolf Steiner for his present incarnation. From the very beginning he was surrounded by the most modern aspects of civilization; from the first hour of his physical existence his environment was shaped by the railway and the telegraph. He was born on 27 February 1861 at Kraljevec[1] which is now in [Austro]-Hungary. He spent only the first 18 months there, on what was known as the Mura Island, followed by six months at a location[2] near Vienna. Then came the move to a place[3] on the border between Lower Austria and Styria in the midst of the hilly Austrian-Styrian region which will make a profound impression on the soul of a child who is receptive to such things.

His father[4] was a lesser official on the Austrian Southern Railway. The family had an ongoing struggle with conditions which cannot be described otherwise than as a 'struggle with the poor pay of such lowly railway officials'. The parents—this must be expressly stated to avoid any misunderstandings—were always prepared to spend their last pennies for the welfare of their children; only not very many such 'last pennies' were available.

Before the boy's eyes—you could say at every moment—were on the one hand the Styrian-Austrian mountains looking down in the distance, frequently sparkling in wonderful sunshine and oftentimes covered in majestic snowfields. One's soul rejoiced in the vegetation and other natural conditions of the area which, lying at the foot of the Schneeberg and Sonnwendstein, is perhaps one of the most beautiful spots of the Austrian landscape. This was one aspect of the impressions surrounding the boy. The other was the fact that at every moment one could turn one's attention to the most up-to-date achievements of civilization: the railway, in the running of which his father was involved, and all that telegraphy was already contributing to modern transport. The boy was of course not in any way surrounded by conditions of urban life. The village where he grew up, and in which the railway station was located, was small; the only modern impression it had to offer was a spinning mill, which meant that there was the permanent presence of a truly up-to-date branch of industry.

All these aspects must be mentioned because they did indeed imbue the boy's soul forces in an inspiring and challenging way. The environment was not of the city, yet city conditions certainly had a bearing on this remote place. Not only was the Semmering Railway[5] quite nearby, a skilfully constructed mountain railway which of course influenced the area, but not far off were also the springs from which at that time Vienna's water supply was taken.[6] In addition the whole locality was popular with those who came from Vienna and other Austrian towns to spend their summer holidays in this part of the mountain region, although of course in the 1860s such places were not as overcrowded

The station at Brunn am Gebirge; Rudolf Steiner's father is second from right.

with holidaymakers as they came to be later on. Even as a child one became acquainted with them and even made friends with some, thus coming more closely into contact with all that was going on in the city. It was as though the city were casting its influence even as far afield as this small village.

Those with some psychological insight will understand that certain other impressions could also be gained, namely how antiquated, traditional religious attitudes can begin to erode within the confines of a small village. There was a priest[7] in the village where the boy was growing up. Of course I shall not mention any names or other details which might cause offence or be hurtful to someone. In descriptions such as this one often has to speak of individuals who are still alive or whose descendants are still living, so I shall endeavour to speak as frankly as possible while avoiding any mention of names. In this village there was a priest whose only influence on my family consisted in baptizing my sister and brother;[8] there was no need for him to baptize me since this had already happened at Kraljevec. Otherwise he was looked upon as a somewhat comical figure by the residents at the station where the boy I am talking about was growing up and also by the people from the spinning mill who used the station where the arrival of a train was always a great event. The boy overheard people talking not very respectfully about 'our Pfarrer Nazl' [from his name, Ignatz].

On the other hand there was another priest[9] in a neighbouring village who often came to our house. This other priest had thoroughly fallen out firstly with 'Pfarrer Nazl' and secondly with all the people he was connected with through his work. This was the person who spoke in front of Rudolf Steiner in his earliest childhood about matters which even then were termed 'Jesuitical', using the loosest language imaginable in the hearing of the four or five-year-old about goings-on in the church. He considered himself to be very much a liberal, and he was greatly appreciated in our house because he was by nature an independent thinker. The boy was highly amused by a tale he once heard told by this priest. A visit by the bishop had been announced, an event which in a small village generally called for a great deal of preparation. Yet it so happened that our liberal-minded priest had to be fetched from his bed and told to hurry because the bishop was already waiting in the church. In short, such conditions could only give rise to something with which perhaps only Austrians are familiar: a certain lack of concern, a degree of indifference towards the traditions of religion. Although one did not bother about such things, one did, at the same time, entertain an interest, culturally and historically, in odd characters like this priest who was late for his meeting with the bishop and thereby caused a stir. No one knew why he had become a priest in the first place, for he never mentioned matters normally of interest to such people. Instead he frequently spoke about his favourite dumplings, and all kinds of things that had happened to him. He used to rail at the ecclesiastical authorities and recount what he had to endure on account of them. This 'reverend father' certainly never manifested any kind of religious fanaticism.

The boy only attended the local primary school for a short while. On account of a personal disagreement between his father and the teacher he was soon removed from the village school and given some lessons in the station office by his father during the intervals between the arrival and departure of the trains.

Then, when the boy was eight or nine years old, his father

was transferred to another station[10] on the Hungarian side of the border between Austria and Hungary. But before speaking about this transfer we must first mention something else which was of the utmost significance and importance for the life of the boy Rudolf Steiner.

In certain respects the boy was something of an embarrassment to his family if only because he had an inborn sense of freedom. If asked to do something with which he did not entirely agree he was inclined to disregard the request. For example he avoided greeting or speaking to certain personages who were his father's superiors and who also came to the village for their summer holidays. He made himself scarce and did not want to join in the subservient behaviour which is of course quite natural and against which there is no reason to complain. I mention simply as a quirk of his nature the fact that he wanted to avoid such things, which he did by withdrawing to the small waiting room where he occupied himself trying to fathom puzzling matters concerning a picture book with figures you could move by pulling strings at the bottom of the pages and which told the story of a character well known in Austria, and especially in Vienna, called 'Staberl'.[11]

Something else also happened to the boy in that waiting room. He was sitting alone on one of the seats. The stove stood in one corner, and there was a door in the wall set back from the stove. The boy was sitting in another corner which gave him a view of the door and the stove. He was still very young. As he sat there the door opened. He found it quite natural that a person entered, a woman whom he had never seen but who looked remarkably like a member of his family. The woman came in through the door and stepped to the middle of the room where she made some gestures and also spoke. Her words might be rendered as follows: 'Strive now and later on to do as much for me as you can!' She remained there for a while, still making gestures of a kind which, once seen, the soul can never forget; then she moved to the stove and disappeared into it.

This incident made a very strong impression on the boy. He had no one in the family whom he could have told about such a thing because, even then, if he had mentioned it he would have been severely scolded for his foolish superstition.

After this incident the following occurred. From that day the boy's father, who was ordinarily a very cheerful man, became rather sad, and the boy could tell that his father did not want to talk about what was troubling him. A few days later, when another member of the family had prepared the ground, what had happened became clear. In a village which for the people at the time would have seemed to be some distance away from the station, a close family member had taken her own life at the very hour when the figure had appeared to the small boy in the waiting room. The boy had neither seen this relation nor had he heard much about her because he was rather inclined—this has to be said—not to listen to what was being talked about by others. Such things went in at one ear and out again at the other, so that he had not actually taken in much of what was being said. He therefore did not know much about the person who had committed suicide. The occurrence made a great impression on the boy for there could be no doubt at all that it was the spirit of that person who had visited him in order to lay upon him the task of doing something for her in the period immediately following her death. Moreover the connections of this spiritual occurrence with the events on the physical plane, as described just now, revealed themselves quite clearly in the ensuing days.

Well, someone who has an experience like this in early childhood,[12] and tries to understand it as best he may in accordance with the disposition of his soul, will know henceforth—if he has experienced it consciously—how one lives in the spiritual worlds. And since I intend to speak only when immediately necessary about how the spiritual worlds shine through into the physical, let me add here: It was from this occurrence onward that there began for the boy a life of soul in which not only the worlds of the external trees and the external mountains but also those worlds which lie behind them can be in touch with the human soul. From about that moment onward the boy lived with the spirits of nature which can be observed so well in such regions; he lived in the same way with the creative beings existing behind the foreground as he did with all that belongs to the external world.

After the transfer, already mentioned, of his father to the border between Austria and Hungary to a village just inside Hungary, the boy began to attend the local village school. It was a village school of the old-fashioned kind in which boys and girls were still taught together as a matter of course. What it was possible to learn in that village school—not a great deal anyway—was not fully effective for the boy with whom we are concerned for the simple reason that the excellent teacher[13]—he was indeed excellent within the prevailing limitations—had a special liking for drawing. And since quite early on the boy turned out to be good at drawing, this teacher simply removed him from the classroom during reading and writing lessons and settled him in his own small room where he had to draw all the time. Quite soon he had succeeded in producing rather a nice portrait—so some people said—of one of Hungary's most eminent political personages, namely Count Széchenyi.[14]

There was of course a priest[15] in that village, too, who visited the school every week. But once again the boy learnt very little about religious affairs from him because, it has to be said, the subject was of no particular concern to him. Religion was not mentioned much at home where it was of little interest. One day, though, the priest came to the school with a small diagram of the Copernican theory which he explained to a number of boys and girls who, he assumed, would be interested. So although the boy learnt nothing about religion from that priest he did, through him, gain quite a good understanding of the Copernican system.

The village where all this was happening was situated in a locality with very special features where once again weighty political and cultural changes were under way. This was the time when Hungary was beginning to develop nationalistic sentiments so that, particularly in border areas, there was considerable turmoil among various nationalities, but especially between the Magyar and German populations. A great deal could be learnt about significant cultural matters, even without being able to categorize everything properly, so that here, too, the boy was brought into contact with utterly up-to-date affairs.

Something that has led to considerable misunderstandings[16] is the fact that, like the other schoolboys in the village, the lad was obliged to act as an altar-boy in the village church—although only for a very brief period. The boys were simply told who was to ring the bells and who had to don altar-boy vestments and assist the priest on any given day. It did not take long before the boy's father insisted—on very curious grounds—that he did not want his son to continue assisting the priest. For various reasons the boy could not always avoid arriving late at the church, and his father did not want him to be beaten as the other boys were when they rang the bells belatedly. So he succeeded in withdrawing his son from that particular duty.

There were also other rather interesting goings on at the time. The priest was not particularly strongly attached to his office, although—unlike the individual mentioned earlier—he did not draw attention to this fact. But he was a fanatical Magyar patriot, and he thought it prudent—as even the boy was able to notice—to act in opposition to something which arose in the village at that time. Once again the boy had an excellent opportunity to observe cultural and historical developments in the making. An acrimonious conflict had broken out between the priest and the Freemasons whose lodge had been established in this village which lay on the Hungarian side of the border,[17] the type of area rather favoured by Freemasonry. In addition to justified criticisms, the local Freemasons were making incredibly exaggerated accusations against the Church. So even if one was still quite young one had ample opportunity to become acquainted with the complaints being made against Church affairs, including some that were quite justified.

Certain things which are not apt to arouse great respect for the Church in a young boy should perhaps not be mentioned in a subsequent publication; nevertheless, one example shall be mentioned here. The boy was able to observe something that did not greatly contribute to his reverence for ecclesiastical tradition. A farmer's son from the village had succeeded in becoming a priest which, of course, made the local peasants very proud. He had become a Cistercian, and a special festival was laid on because the whole village was proud that a farmer's son had been so successful. The boy saw what was happening. After five or six years the priest had been given a parish of his own, but he came back to visit his home village now and again. And people observed that a vehicle pushed by that priest together with a woman in peasant clothing grew ever heavier. The vehicle was a pram, and each year brought one more child needing to be pushed in it. From the very first visit of the priest to his home village a remarkable increase in the size of his family occurred, which seemed an ever stranger 'amplification' of his celibacy as the years went by. Perhaps one may remark that this was not the best way to ensure the boy's respect for ecclesiastical traditions.

Now to something else. When he was about eight years old the boy found among the books of the teacher mentioned earlier a geometry textbook by Močnik[18] which was frequently used in Austrian schools at the time. All by himself he began to study geometry, immersing himself in the subject with great pleasure.

It came to be regarded as a matter of course in the boy's family that his education should enable him to take up a modern profession. Every effort was therefore made to ensure that he would not turn to any other but a modern profession. As a result of this he was sent not to a *Gymnasium* [which would specialize in classical studies] but to a *Real-schule* [which would specialize in science and technology]. As he did not attend a *Gymnasium* he had no schooling which might have prepared him for a clerical profession. At that time in Austria the *Realschule* presented no possibility whatsoever which might have provided a basis for a clerical career later on. Conversely, his talent for drawing and his interest in geometry qualified him nicely for the *Realschule*.

For him it was languages, including the German language, which were the problem. Until he was 14 or 15 he made the most stupid mistakes in German when doing his schoolwork; it was only the content which helped him counterbalance his many mistakes in grammar and spelling. It is appropriate to mention here the reason why the boy about whom we are speaking came to disregard certain aspects of grammar and spelling even in his mother-tongue. It was a symptom of a particular type of inner soul life which lacked, in a certain way, the ability to link up directly with the dry-as-dust aspects of life in the physical world. On occasion this showed in quite bizarre ways.

For example, when he was still in the village school, before moving on to the *Realschule*, the children had to write festive New Year or birthday greetings on pretty paper to parents and others. Then they had to learn these greetings by heart before the teacher rolled them up and fixed them in paper rings. The children then handed the rolls to the recipients while reciting the contents. You will remember the priest who amused the boy so much by taking up cudgels against the Freemasons. (Since the founder of the local lodge was Jewish, one of the priest's thundering declarations from the pulpit had been the announcement that the way to become a bad person was to become either a Jew or a Freemason, which made everyone roar with laughter.) Well, that priest had a young boy living at his residence—please do not think that there was anything improper in this—who also attended the school and had to write down his festive greetings. It so happened that the boy Rudolf Steiner glanced at the draft for the other boy's greetings and saw that he had written 'From your affectionate nephew'. At the time, the boy Rudolf Steiner did not know what a 'nephew' was as he sometimes did not connect words with what they meant. But he did have a feeling for the sounds of words, for what one can learn from them through their sounds. So from the sound of the word 'nephew' he gathered that this was something especially heartfelt when you used it in signing a greeting for one of your relatives. So he also began to sign his note to his father and mother by writing 'From your affectionate nephew'. He only realized what a 'nephew' was once the meaning of the word was explained to him. He was ten years old when this incident occurred.

The boy then began attending the *Realschule* in the neighbouring town.[19] It was not always easy to get to the school. His parents' financial situation meant that lodging in the town was out of the question. However, the school was only an hour's walk from the village where he lived. In winter it occasionally happened that the railway line was not snowed under, so the boy was then able to take the train to school. But the railway was frequently closed by snow just when the walk to school, which led across fields, was least pleasant. It then often took the boy an hour and a half to wade to school through knee-deep snow. And in the evening the only way to go home was on foot.[20]

Looking back now to that boy, for whom it was exceedingly strenuous to get to and from school, I cannot help thinking that the degree of good health I now enjoy may be attributable to that strenuous wading through knee-deep snow and the other exertions connected with attendance at the *Realschule*. During the first four years of his attendance at the school there was in the town a good woman[21] who gave the boy a meal and somewhere to rest during the midday break, so that at least the problem of finding something to eat was mitigated. As this woman's husband was employed at the locomotive factory the boy also came into contact with the most modern aspects of civilization. He had ample opportunity to learn a great deal about conditions at that industrial site which was so important in its day. In this way those most modern conditions of industry also had a bearing on the boy's life.

There were many things connected with the school which greatly interested the boy. First there was the headmaster, a most remarkable man.[22] He was thoroughly immersed in the scientific thought of the time and was making every effort in the late 1860s and early 1870s to elaborate a kind of universal system. The boy learnt of the headmaster's efforts through a thesis he had written entitled 'The force of attraction as an effect of movement' which launched straight in with an intensive exposition of the mathematical process of integration. So the boy now made intense efforts to penetrate the things he did not understand, reading everything he could find. To some extent he understood the thesis to signify that the forces of the world, including the force of attraction, could be explained as originating out of movement. The urge now arose in the boy to learn as quickly as possible enough about mathematics to enable him to penetrate these ideas. This was not easy since in order to understand such things one first had to learn a good deal about geometry.

Something else arose as well. There was also an excellent physics and mathematics teacher[23] at the *Realschule*. He, too, had written a thesis which attracted the boy's attention. This was an exceptionally interesting treatise about the theory of probability and life insurance. Thus the boy received a second impulse, namely to find out how one can insure people on the basis of probability calculations, which was very clearly explained in that essay.

There was also a third teacher who should be mentioned, the geometry teacher.[24] The boy had the good fortune to be taught by him from the second school year onwards. From him he learned what later led him to projective geometry and the geometrical drawing connected with it, in other words the necessary mathematics as well as the freehand drawing. This teacher of geometry was different from the headmaster and from the one who wrote the thesis about life insurance. The manner in which he presented geometry and instructed his pupils in the use of compasses and ruler was extremely practical, and it has to be said that it was because of the way this teacher taught that the boy became entirely enthusiastic about geometry and also geometrical construction with compasses and ruler. The teacher's clear and practical way of teaching was enhanced by the fact that he regarded textbooks as merely a bit of incidental entertainment. What he taught was dictated in his own words and drawn by him on the blackboard. The children copied this and thus made their own 'textbooks'; there was nothing else they needed to know apart from what they themselves had put into their own exercise-books. It was good to learn by participating in this way. Other subjects, by contrast, often involved excellent instructions on how to sleep through the whole lesson.

In the third class of the *Realschule* the boy often had lessons with the mathematics and physics teacher who had written the thesis about probability and life insurance. He was an excellent teacher for mathematics and physics. And whenever the man who has grown from that boy feels something light up in his soul upon thinking about that excellent teacher of mathematics and physics, his inclination is always to lay in spirit a tributary wreath at his feet. The boy now became truly enthusiastic about mathematics and physics, so at a comparatively young age he was already able to work with the excellent textbooks for self-instruction in mathematics by H.B. Lübsen,[25] which were then much better known than they are nowadays. With the help of Lübsen's books, while still comparatively young, the boy also came to understand what the headmaster had written about 'The force of attraction as an effect of movement' and also what the other teacher had written about probability and life insurance. He was delighted to reach an understanding of these matters as time went on.

Another feature of the boy's life at that time was the fact that he had no money to pay for having his schoolbooks bound. But one of his father's assistants taught him book-binding,[26] so he was able to bind his own books during the school holidays. I think it is important to mention this because learning something as practical as bookbinding at that early age was most important for the boy's development. And something else occurred at this time as well. It was the period when Austria introduced the new system of weights and measures which was to replace the old system of inches, feet, pounds and hundredweights with the metric system of metres and kilograms. The boy shared the enthusiasm of people in all walks of life when they stopped calculating in feet, pounds and hundredweights and began to replace these with metres and kilograms. The most-read book,[27] which he always carried about in his pocket, was the one, now for-gotten, on the new system of weights and measures. He was soon able to recite what a number of pounds amounted to in kilograms and a number of feet in metres, for the book contained long tables of equivalents.

Another person who played a part in the boy's life should not be forgotten, a physician[28] and very open-minded man.

The college of teachers at the Landes-Oberrealschule *in Wiener-Neustadt 1873. No. 9 Georg Kusak, geometry teacher; No. 12 Dr Hugo von Gilm, chemistry and physics teacher.*

The boy had known him since the family's residency at the first railway station—where he had had the mystical experience. This physician's view of life—please do not take this amiss—was what one might call somewhat wide-ranging. Although he was a very good physician, he had his peculiarities which led to situations like the following. On one occasion the points guard at the station had a violent toothache. Although not resident at the station, the physician was responsible for the railway staff. Being in a hurry, he telegraphed the station to say that he would be arriving on such-and-such a train but did not want to leave it and would therefore extract the tooth while the train waited. So that is what happened. But once the train had departed the guard came and said, 'Well, he's pulled out a good tooth, but the other one doesn't hurt any more either!' On another occasion the same guard had a very bad stomach ache, and the physician had a similar idea. This time the train was an express and would not be stopping at the station. So he ordered the guard to stand on the platform and stick out his tongue, and he would telegraph the remedy from the train's next stop. The guard duly positioned himself on the platform and stuck out his tongue at the passing train, and the physician telephoned his prescription from the next stop. Such was that man's 'wide-ranging view of life'. Nevertheless he was a sensitive and exceptionally kind-hearted individual.

The boy had long since finished studying the new system of weights and measures and come to grips with integral and differential calculus. But he knew nothing about Goethe or Schiller other than what was contained in school textbooks, a few poems but nothing else about German or any other literature. He retained, however, a singular and natural affection for that physician. In the town where he attended school he passed with a feeling of reverence beneath his windows, where without being noticed he was able to observe him wearing his green eyeshade, immersed in his books. Once, during a visit to the village just mentioned, it so happened that the physician invited the boy to pay him a visit sometime. So he called on him one day, and the physician became an affectionate adviser, lending him important works of German literature—sometimes in annotated editions. He never sent him on his away without a warm word and always received him just as affectionately when he returned the books. So in addition to the other aspect I have already described, that physician remained one of the most highly respected among the persons known to the boy. Much of what he absorbed by way of literature and whatever is connected with it entered his soul through that physician.

Something rather remarkable also happened to the boy. On account of the excellent geometry teacher he had become very enthusiastic about projective geometry, and this led to something which had never before happened in his school, or indeed in any other school. This was that from the fourth class onwards his work in projective geometry and drawing[29] received the highest possible mark. Normally the highest mark, which was difficult to attain, was 'Excellent'. Yet the boy was awarded 'Outstanding'. He did indeed know much more about these things than about literature and similar subjects.

Certain other aspects also prevailed at the school. For example for the duration of several classes the history teacher was a very boring sort of man and it was exceedingly difficult to listen to him. All he did was present the content of the textbook, and it was easier to absorb this by reading the book itself afterwards. So the boy worked out a cunning scheme which made use of his inclinations at that time. He never had much money, but after saving the odd pennies that came his way over many weeks he managed to scrape a small sum together. As his good karma would have it, this was the time when Reclam began to publish their *Universal-Bibliothek*,[30] and among the first volumes to be brought out were, for example, the works of Kant.

Kant's *Critique of Pure Reason* was the first he bought. He was 14 or 15 years old. The teacher's history lessons bored him dreadfully; but on the other hand he had little spare time owing to the large amount of homework to be done each evening for the next morning. The only useful spare time he had were the history teacher's very boring lessons, so he worked out a way of taking advantage of these. Since he had learnt the skill of bookbinding he took the history textbook to pieces and made a neat job of re-binding it with the pages of Kant's *Critique of Pure Reason* inserted in it. And while the teacher recited the contents of the textbook up at the front, the boy read Kant's *Critique of Pure Reason* with great attentiveness. He managed to penetrate Kant's *Critique of Pure Reason* with deep interest at the age of 15 and was then able to continue with other works by the same author.

Without boasting it can be said that by the age of 16 or 17 the boy had succeeded in absorbing Kant's works in so far as they were contained in Reclam's *Universal-Bibliothek*. In addition to reading during the history lessons he also had time during the holidays. He devoted himself enthusiastically to the study of Kant and found a new world opening up to him from the physical plane.

The boy's years at the *Realschule* were drawing to a close.[31] Behind him lay an entirely modern school education. Two more aspects should still be highlighted. During the later classes there was also an excellent chemistry teacher[32] who, rather than talking too much, only said what was strictly necessary. All kinds of apparatus were spread out along a counter several metres in length. The teacher demonstrated everything, even the most complicated experiments, while making only the most essential comments. After yet another such interesting lesson the pupils used to ask: 'Herr Doktor'—he preferred this address to 'Herr Professor'—'will the next lesson be experiments or exams?' As a rule the terse answer was, 'Experiments,' whereupon everyone was delighted. Tests usually took place only during the final two lessons before reports were written. But since all the boys had paid good attention and worked well—and also because he was such an excellent teacher—they always knew enough. We may add that he was the brother of the Austrian-Tyrolean poet Hermann von Gilm,[33] an important lyricist, who has recently become better known again in Austria. I am making an exception in mentioning this name of someone who no longer dwells among us since nothing but good can be said of him.

The other aspect still to be mentioned is that in a castle near the village there lived a man, Count Chambord,[34] who was a pretender to a European throne which he was never able to ascend on account of the political situation at the time. He was a great benefactor in the neighbourhood, and many things were known in the village about what went on in that castle belonging to the pretender to a throne. Of course the boy never had an opportunity to meet the Count who was very much alive in the talk of the whole countryside. Although he was a person with whom not many were able to agree, nevertheless his presence brought the influence of important political conditions, with which the boy therefore became familiar, right into the village.

There are other things to be mentioned as well. Having had the flames of his interest fanned by Kant, the boy gradually began to turn his mind to other philosophical subjects, so now he spent his meagre means on works of psychology and logic. He was especially attracted to books by Lindner[35] which, as far as psychology was concerned, were a good source of information; and from there, even before he left the *Realschule*, he followed leads to the philosophy of Herbart[36] with which he became quite familiar.

One problem did arise from this, however. The German language teacher, otherwise an excellent man who merited much praise for what he accomplished on behalf of the school, was not at all pleased with the boy's choice of reading matter because it tempted him to write frightfully long essays which sometimes even filled an entire exercise book. After passing the *Abitur*,[37] the final exam to be taken upon leaving the school, when it was customary for the pupils to have a final meeting with the teachers, this teacher said to the boy, 'Well, well, you were my most prolific phrase-monger! I was always filled with dread when you handed in an essay.' Once, when the boy had used the expression 'psychological free-dom', the teacher had given him the following advice: 'You certainly appear to have a philosophical library at home. Take my advice and don't spend too much time studying those books.'

The boy was especially interested in a lecture on 'Pessimism' given by a teacher in that small town. It should be added that in the higher classes at the *Realschule* the history lessons were excellent. The boy thus received a thorough grounding in the history of the Thirty Years' War. He had

Class photograph around 1876. Rudolf Steiner: second row from the back, far right.

obtained possession of Rotteck's[38] *Weltgeschichte* which impressed him greatly on account of the warmth with which the first volumes of that 'World History' were written.

Another significant fact is that the boy attended only the first four years of religious instruction, which were compulsory.[39] Having been released from compulsory attendance after the end of the fourth year, he no longer took this subject. Due to the situation in his family he was also never confirmed, and remains unconfirmed to this day. You do not have before you a person who has been confirmed. It was taken for granted among those around him as he grew up that one did not participate in religious customs.

By contrast, one of the physics tests set in the *Abitur* examination made a deep impression on him. It was so up-to-date that this was surely the first time it had been posed in Austrian schools. He was asked to explain the telephone, which had just begun to gain ground at the time. He had to make a sketch on the blackboard showing how telephone calls are made from one terminal to another.

When he had finished school, the boy became very keen on a number of philosophical questions. He had completed his final examinations, and his father had applied for a transfer to a different railway station closer to Vienna[40] so that his son would be able to attend the university. It was during the holiday following the *Abitur* exam that the boy began to feel a truly profound wish to find some answers to philosophical questions. This wish could only be fulfilled in one way. Over the years he had collected a considerable number of books. These he now took to the second-hand bookseller who gave him a tidy sum in return. He immediately spent it all on books of philosophy. So now he was able to read more works by Kant, for example his dissertation of 1763 *Attempt to Introduce the Concept of Negative Value into the Wisdom of the World*, or his *Dreams of a Spiritual Seer Elucidated by the Dreams of Metaphysics*, both of which mention Swedenborg. Not only Kant but all [philosophical] literature could be studied through representative works of individual authors such as Hegel, Schelling, Fichte and their followers, for example Karl Leonhard Reinhold,[41] and by Darwin and so on. He even considered a philosopher who is no longer held in much esteem today, the Kantian Traugott Krug.[42]

The time had now come for the boy to go to university. Of course this had to be a technical university since he had no general background in the humanities or classical subjects. So he registered at the Technical University of Vienna[43] where in the first years he read chemistry, physics, zoology, botany, biology, mineralogy, geology, mathematics, geometry and pure mechanics. He also attended lectures on the history of German literature given by a man who had a profound connection with his life, the lecturer on German Literature at the Technical University, Karl Julius Schröer.[44]

In the boy's first year at university [1879/80] something very special occurred. Through a singular chain of events he came into contact with a remarkable man. This was a person without any formal learning who nevertheless possessed comprehensive and most profound knowledge and wisdom. Let us call him by his actual first name, 'Felix'.[45] He lived with his peasant family in a remote and isolated mountain village; his living room was filled with mystical and esoteric literature and he himself had penetrated deeply into mystical and esoteric wisdom. Most of his time was spent gathering plants. He collected all kinds of plants throughout the surrounding neighbourhoods and—as became evident on the rare occasions when one was permitted to accompany him on his solitary wanderings—he was able to explain the inner nature of every plant according to its spiritual background. He was a man of infinite spiritual depths.

Significant conversations were had with him as he travelled to town, on the same train as the boy, with his bundle on his back full of plants of every kind which he had collected and dried. Important talks took place with this man known in Austria as a *Dürrkräutler*, someone who collects and dries herbs and plants before supplying them to the apothecaries. That was the man's outer occupation, but his inner calling was of course quite different. We should not forget to mention that he loved everything in the world and only showed bitterness—this is mentioned solely for the historical record—when the conversation turned to clerical matters and to what was inflicted, also on him, from that quarter; towards this he was not favourably disposed.

Something else soon followed. My Felix was, as it were, simply the herald of another personage[46] who had a way of stimulating in the boy's soul, as it already stood within the spiritual world, those regular, systematic things with which one must be familiar in the spiritual world. That personage, too, was exceedingly averse to every form of clericalism and of course had nothing to do with such things. His way of proceeding was to take the works of Fichte as the basis for certain considerations which generated seeds that came to fruition in the book *An Outline of Esoteric Science* which the man the boy had become later wrote. Certain aspects which led to that book[47] were considered in connection with Fichte's writings.

The excellent personage in question was as obscure as Felix in his outer occupation. As a starting point he used a book[48] little known to the world at large and also frequently suppressed in Austria for its anti-clerical tendency. Yet it was very useful as a means of encouraging the discovery of spiritual paths. Those singular streams which flow through the esoteric world, and which can only be recognized if one bears in mind an upward and a downward flowing double stream,[49] appeared at that time in a very lively way before the boy's soul. He was introduced in this way to esoteric things before he had read the second part of *Faust*. There is no need for more to be said here about the esoteric training of the young man the boy had grown up to be. He kept all he learned within his soul; he experienced it all within himself as he continued to tread the external path of his life.

Initially Karl Julius Schröer's historical lectures on 'German literature since Goethe's first appearance' encouraged him to study Goethe's *Theory of Colour* and the second part of *Faust* as an 18 or 19-year-old youth. At the same time he studied Herbart's philosophy, particularly the *Metaphysics*.[50] The youth experienced an unusual disappointment in this connection. Having already become acquainted with a good deal of philosophy, he had certain reasons of his own for admiring Herbart's philosophy in particular. He had therefore been eagerly looking forward to making the acquaintance of Robert Zimmermann,[51] who was one of its most prominent proponents. This turned out to be a great disappointment because one's estimation of Herbart's philosophy was much dampened by Zimmermann's intolerable lecturing manner, although he was otherwise a very clever man.

On the other hand the youth received a very helpful impulse from a historian with whom he later became acquainted, namely Ottokar Lorenz.[52] He was not overly inclined to attend all the courses at the Technical University with pedantic regularity although he did participate in everything. In his spare time he had also listened in at tutorials given at the University of Vienna, by Robert Zimmermann on 'Practical Philosophy' and by Franz Brentano[53] on 'Psychology'. Brentano's lectures did not impress the youth as much as his books, all of which he later came to know thoroughly. The liberal ideas of the free thinker Ottokar Lorenz did impress him in this period known as the 'Austrian liberal era'. He was certainly able to make an impression on young minds, using the most acerbic language, railing with many examples against whatever needed criticizing. But he was entirely honest in all this; having commented on some 'ticklish' matter he would end by saying: 'I had to paint this in rather rosy tints because if I were to speak plainly about every aspect the public prosecutor would be waiting here next time.'

An anecdote—in so far as anecdotes are true: actually, they are truer than true—an anecdote was told about the same Ottokar Lorenz. A colleague of his, who lectured on the auxiliary sciences connected with history, was to examine a favourite student in connection with the attainment of his doctorate, and he asked Lorenz to conduct the examination with him. The student was able to give the correct information, for example, as to when the dot on the i first appeared in a papal document. Since the student had immediately given the correct answer, Lorenz also wanted to put a question: 'Would the candidate like to tell me when the pope in question was born?' The candidate did not know. So he was asked the date of the pope's death. Again, he didn't know. And when he was asked whether he knew anything else about the pope, the reply was negative once more. The professor whose favourite student this was then said: 'But my dear candidate, you appear to be surrounded by an impermeable fog today!' Whereupon Lorenz exclaimed: 'Well, professor, this is your favourite pupil. Who do you suppose created the impermeable fog which now surrounds the candidate?' This is the kind of thing that happened from time to time.

Lorenz was a great favourite among all the students at Vienna University. He was even chancellor there for a year; and it was customary for someone who had been chancellor to act as vice-chancellor during the following year. His successor as chancellor was an extremely right-wing cleric, deeply unpopular with the students who heckled him mercilessly when he lectured. His subject was ecclesiastical law, and Lorenz was his most emphatic critic. The man could barely set foot in the university without a frightful commotion ensuing, and it was then up to the vice-chancellor to come and restore order. As soon as Lorenz appeared on the scene the students began to cheer him. So Ottokar Lorenz drew himself up and declared: 'Your applause leaves me cold. However different the two of us might be, if you treat my colleague in this way and yet raise a cheer for me when I appear, then I say to you that from the point of view of scholarship I am not worthy to tie this man's shoelace; I recoil from your applause which means nothing to me!' '*Pereat, pereat*', shouted the students, and his popularity was gone.

Lorenz subsequently moved to Jena, and the person speaking to you now met with him again on many occasions. He is no longer present on the physical plane. He was an excellent man, and I can still see in my mind's eye every detail of him lecturing[54] on how the activities of Charles Augustus related to the rest of German politics. In the following year, again at the meeting of the Goethe Society, as we sat together and chatted about the lecture he had given the year before, his fundamental honesty emerged when he said, 'What I said last year about Charles Augustus' relationship with German politics—well, that was a big blunder!' The man was always ready to admit his mistakes.

In addition to numerous others who made an impression on the youth at that time, let us mention an excellent man who died soon afterwards. The youth attended the tutorials on the history of physics which he gave at the Technical University. This was Edmund Reitlinger[55] who collaborated on a book about Kepler and also gave excellent accounts depicting the evolution of physics through the ages.

Important incentives also came from Karl Julius Schröer who influenced his students not only through lectures but also in a tutorial course on 'Speaking in public and clarity in writing'. The students had to hold forth in lectures and learn how to structure such lectures properly. This also enabled some to catch up with matters of sentence construction which they had missed out on earlier. In short, we were given a thorough grounding in speaking and writing. I can vividly remember the lectures given by the youth with whom we are concerned here. His first was about the importance of Lessing, especially his *Laocoön*; the second was on Kant with special reference to the question of freedom. Another talk was about Herbart and his ethics; and the fourth practice lecture discussed pessimism.

During one session of those tutorials on 'Speaking in public and clarity in writing' a fellow-student[56] opened a discussion about Schopenhauer, and the youth about whom we are speaking said during the debate: 'I greatly admire Schopenhauer, but if the conclusions he reaches are correct I would rather be a wooden board like the one on which I am standing than a living being.' This was the mood of his soul at the time, which made him want to oppose that enthusiastic supporter of Schopenhauer. That he would today no longer wish to reject him is demonstrated by the fact that he himself has since edited an edition of Schopenhauer's works[57] in which he sought to do justice to the philosopher's views.

There was in those days a student society[58] at the Technical University, and the youth of whom we are speaking was given the post of treasurer. He fulfilled his duties in that capacity for some of the time, but otherwise he was more concerned with the library. This was firstly because he was interested in philosophy, but secondly because he longed to become more familiar with cultural life in general. His longing in this respect was very great, but he had no means

Rudolf Steiner as a student in Vienna, around 1882

with which to purchase books. After a while he came to be taken for granted as the librarian of that society.

When a book was needed, he wrote a 'begging letter' to the author on behalf of the society telling him that the students would be most grateful if he would donate a copy. For the most part these begging letters were indeed graciously answered with the gift of a book. In this way the most important philosophical works of the age found their way to the library where they were read—at least by the one who had written the begging letter.

The person in question was thus able to discover not only the *Erkenntnistheorie* of Johannes Volkelt[59] and the works of Richard Falckenberg[60] but also the books of Helmholtz[61] as well as works of history. Many authors sent their books; Kuno Fischer[62] himself once donated a volume of his *Geschichte der neueren Philosophie*. One writer, Baron Hellenbach,[63] even sent copies of all his works after receiving a begging letter. There was thus ample opportunity to become acquainted with philosophical and cultural books as well as literary and historical works. And it was possible to deepen one's insight in other realms as well.

Through personal and ever closer ties of friendship with Karl Julius Schröer, who was not only an expert on Goethe but also a profoundly important commentator on his works, it then came about that the youth, too, began to take an interest in Goethe's ideas, especially those pertaining to the sciences. After much effort, Schröer succeeded in finding a way of publishing a number of essays with a physics component which the young man had written in connection with the Theory of Colour.[64]

He was then approached with the offer to collaborate on the comprehensive edition of Goethe's works being prepared at the time by Joseph Kürschner[65] in the series *Kürschners National-Literatur*. He was allocated the scientific works of Goethe and was also invited to write the introduction to that section. Once the first volume of 'Goethe's Scientific Writings with Introductions by Rudolf Steiner' had been published, he felt impelled to present on that foundation the sources of Goethe's thinking from which, after all, the whole Goethean view of the world shown there had arisen. So between the publication of the first and second volumes he wrote *Goethe's Theory of Knowledge*.[66] In the early 1880s he had also written several other essays.[67] One of these, which was published, was entitled 'Auf der Höhe';[68] then there was one on Hermann Hettner,[69] one on Lessing and one about 'Parallels between Shakespeare and Goethe'. All these essays were written around that time.

Rudolf Steiner soon became involved in a great deal of writing through having become a contributor to *Kürschners Deutsche National-Literatur* for which he edited Goethe's scientific writings and wrote detailed introductions. One should point out that just as earlier the student union had backed him, so now the same was done by the Vienna Goethe Society[70] of which Karl Julius Schröer was deputy president. Once the first Goethe volumes had been published, another important event for him was the invitation by Schröer to address a notable gathering, namely the membership of the Goethe Society. The lecture he gave was entitled 'Goethe as the Founder of a New Science of Aesthetics'.[71]

The time arrived when the person whose life circumstances are being described here had progressed beyond his days at university and become a tutor. From the age of 14 onwards he had always given private lessons and taught other boys; and he continued to do this teaching out of necessity, because he had to support himself. During his years at university he was obliged to coach a good many schoolchildren and he was happy to have many pupils who needed extra tuition. This continued when he became a member of the Goethe Society, and it was then that he became tutor in a Viennese family.[72]

It has to be said of this family that with them, once again, the most modern circumstances came to the fore. The father of the family, whose sons were to be educated by Rudolf Steiner, was one of the most distinguished representatives of the cotton trade carried on between Europe and America; and this surely was something that could lead one most deeply into the commercial problems of modern times. He was a decidedly liberal gentleman. And the two women, sisters—whose families shared the house harmoniously—were admirable in their profound understanding on the one hand of childcare and on the other of the idealism which came to expression in Rudolf Steiner's introductions to Goethe's scientific writings and in *A Theory of Knowledge*.

He now had the opportunity to learn about practical psychology in connection with educating several boys. It was practical psychology in that he was free to take initiatives on his own in all matters pertaining to the education of the children because the mother of those boys put complete trust in him. He was entering here upon many years in the post of tutor, and he was able to carry out his duties in this respect in a way which also enabled him to continue with his work on the introduction to Goethe's scientific writings.

Up to this point in time, Rudolf Steiner had completed attendance at the *Realschule* and at Vienna's Technical University. And now his life was involved with the education of boys who were themselves pupils at the *Realschule*, with only one of them attending the *Gymnasium*. Because this one boy was a pupil at the *Gymnasium* the tutor was now obliged to catch up on the curriculum of the *Gymnasium*. This obligation, in his twenty-third year, to catch up with the teaching at the *Gymnasium* by accompanying the boy, was what later on made it possible for him to attain his doctorate.

His education up to his twentieth year had brought him into contact solely with the *Realschule*, which in Austria never prepares an individual for entry into a clerical profession. Indeed, it positively precludes this. Thereafter he had attended the Technical University, which again does not prepare one for a clerical profession, since the subjects one studies there are chemistry, physics, zoology, botany, mechanics in relation to engineering, geology and suchlike, and also modern geometry, namely projective geometry. Side by side with this, during his time at the university, he entered deeply into various philosophical works and finally, as his friendship with Schröer developed, came his approach to the Goethe editions.

Only then did he embark on what might be termed a 'professional' activity, that of tutoring. And since one of the boys was not quite normal, this also involved 'practical psychology'. So during this period the young man was most certainly not attending the Jesuit college at Kalksburg[73] as some people claim to have been the case (nor elsewhere[74] as has recently been presumed). Instead his time was spent as a tutor in a Jewish household in Vienna where he most certainly underwent no instruction that might have led to any Jesuitical activities. The understanding developed by those two women regarding any idealism or any educational maxims applied to the children was in no way conducive to allowing any approach through Jesuitism.

There was only one aspect which might, as it were, have been casting a shadow emanating from the world of Jesuitism. This came about as follows. Schröer made the acquaintance of the Austrian poet Marie Eugenie delle Grazie[75] who lived in the house of a Catholic priest, Laurenz Müllner,[76] who later transferred to the philosophical faculty. In order to see that Müllner had no intention of bringing Jesuitism to bear on her you need only read what Marie Eugenie delle Grazie wrote. But one also met with all kinds of university professors there, among them one who was very knowledgeable about the Semites and the Semitic languages and also had a profound understanding of the Old Testament.[77] He was a thoroughly learned gentleman about whom people said that he 'knew the whole world and another three villages in addition'. But the conversations I had with him and which I found significant were all about Christianity. What this scholar had to say about Christianity at that time referred, for one, to the question of the *conceptio immaculata*, the immaculate conception. I endeavoured to prove to him that there was something entirely inconsistent in this dogma since it was a question not only of Mary's immaculate conception but also of that of her mother, Saint Anna. I said that one would have to follow this further and further back. But this man was quite a free-thinking theologian who was not at all inclined to present himself as '*the* theologian'. So he merely added, 'We can't do that; if we did we'd eventually end up with King David, and then things could get quite tricky.'

This was the tone that prevailed in conversations held in the house of Professor Müllner during delle Grazie's soirées. Müllner was a sarcastic spirit, and the professors were also free-thinking men. Whatever shone over from the other direction actually came from only one individual who tended towards Jesuitism and who subsequently met with a tragic end. He drowned when he was shipwrecked in the Adriatic. That man was an ecclesiastical historian at Vienna University.[78] He spoke little, but what he said was not a good representation of the other element. It was rumoured that he was afraid to leave his house after dark because he thought that was when the Freemasons were out and about. So he was not able to generate much interest in Jesuitism, firstly because he was not a good ecclesiastical historian and secondly because of such gossip. And he did indeed always disappear before darkness fell.

There was also another circumstance which enabled me to become more closely acquainted with Austrian political conditions. That was because I was able to edit the *Deutsche Wochenschrift* which Heinrich Friedjung[79] had founded. This represented a decidedly liberal viewpoint with regard to circumstances in Austria which anyone can study by becoming acquainted with what Friedjung presented. Rudolf Steiner also came into contact with other political matters and personalities. Although his time as editor turned out to be quite brief, it occurred during a very important moment, namely after the Battenberg prince[80] had been driven out of Bulgaria and when the new Prince of Bulgaria was installed. This influenced the picture one was likely to arrive at concerning the cultural and political situation.

During that period a work was published which is rather significant, although some might consider it to be one-sided, namely *Homunkulus* by Robert Hamerling.[81] *Homunkulus* was also especially important for the life of the person about whom we are speaking because he had been acquainted with Hamerling earlier on. Although Rudolf Steiner had been born at Kraljevec, his family came from Lower Austria, the so-called 'Bandlkramerlandl' area,[82] where pedlars went about humping bundles of locally woven ribbons. It was from there that his family came. And as often happens with families whose work takes them all over the place, the boy never returned to Lower Austria. But since he stemmed from the same 'Bandlkramerlandl' as Hamerling he felt some kind of kinship with him. Hamerling was not particularly well understood. But it could be said of him that although his upbringing had not been Jesuitical, nevertheless he had been educated in a monastery, which was not so at all in the case of the person standing here before you. Robert Hamerling was not well known. Once, later on, when he paid a visit to his home region he told the innkeeper at the inn 'that he was Hamerling'. The innkeeper replied, 'Oh, so you're Hamerling are you?'

Steps were taken at the time to send Hamerling a copy of *Goethe's Theory of Knowledge*. What he thought of it can be gleaned from one of the most important chapters in his *Atomistik des Willens*[83] where he discusses the nature of mathematical judgements. It seems to me today that he applies it in a thoroughly original manner. There followed a not very long exchange of letters[84] with Robert Hamerling which was in a specific sense important for Rudolf Steiner. This was because after he had written to Hamerling he received a reply in which that gifted stylist told him that he wrote in an exceptionally attractive and beautiful style and that he had a talent for tellingly describing what he wished to depict. This was exceedingly important for Rudolf Steiner because those were the years in which he lacked confidence in his writing; but thereafter through Robert Hamerling he gained more confidence in the matter of the style he used for his descriptions. It was pointed out earlier that up to his thirteenth or fourteenth year the boy had not been at all competent in grammar and spelling and that it was only the content of his essays which had helped him transcend all those grammatical and orthographical errors.

As the Goethe edition was nearing completion and as he had belatedly acquired the necessary knowledge about the ancient world which he needed for teaching the boy he was educating, the time now came for Rudolf Steiner to approach his doctoral examination.[85] He had also been able to develop a true eye for art and architecture thanks to the fact that great architects[86] were living in Vienna at that time which meant that he had become personally acquainted with them at the University. We may mention that the Votive Church, the Town Hall and the Parliament House, among others, were built in Vienna during that period. This enabled one to contemplate much that had a bearing on art. One might point out that those were the days when fierce arguments arose with ardent admirers of Wagner; the person about whom we are speaking here had to make strenuous efforts to reach an attitude of admiration towards Richard Wagner, an admiration with which you have become acquainted through other descriptions elsewhere.[87]

Rudolf Steiner also at this time became acquainted with a spiritual stream which, although it had come into being earlier, had only now made its appearance in Europe. This was the theosophical orientation which H.P. Blavatsky[88] was promulgating. The person about whom we are speaking should point out that he was perhaps one of the first to purchase the German translations of *Esoteric Buddhism* by A.P. Sinnet[89] and *Light on the Path* by Mabel Collins.[90] He immediately took the latter to the sickbed of a lady who was seriously ill at the time and made suggestions with the intention of helping her to understand it from her point of view. He also presented it to a gentleman whom he was coaching in integral calculus and mathematics, prior to his sitting the Austrian officers' examination, who resided in the house belonging to the family of the very sick lady.

At that time, the Viennese representatives of the theosophical movement also approached me. The person about whom we are speaking entered into a very intimate and friendly relationship with all those who had gathered around Franz Hartmann,[91] recently deceased, and also with other theosophists. This was during the years 1884–85 when the theosophical movement had only just begun to become known. However, it was at the time not possible for the person about whom we are speaking to join the movement, even though he was intimately familiar with it, because the overall conduct and behaviour of the members, what might be termed the artificiality of their comportment, was incompatible with the kind of philosophical exactitude, precision and genuineness anchored in the life of the senses which he had come to embody. This should not be taken to denote any kind of self-commendation. I am more inclined to ascribe it to what we possess in our time as the result of genuine erudition. Whatever else might incur our disapproval in the matter of erudition, we cannot object to the greatest and most keen-sighted logic that may arise from it.

Thus it came about that the one about whom we are speaking became personally acquainted with estimable individuals within the theosophical circle, for example Rosa Mayreder[92] who subsequently turned right away from theosophical tendencies. He became thoroughly familiar with the external history of the whole movement, yet he was unable to have anything to do with it. He only came to a practical application of theosophical ways when he found himself obliged to immerse himself in Goethe's *Tale of the Green Snake and the Beautiful Lily*. In order to make a commentary on this tale he initially concerned himself in a practical way with something which had lived in his soul since his very first occult experience. That was in 1888 after he had become thoroughly acquainted with the theosophical movement without being capable of forming any external attachment to it despite having come to know some estimable individuals within it.

There is also another profound impression which should be mentioned, an impression experienced by the person about whom we are speaking when he visited an art exhibition in Vienna in 1888 where for the first time he saw paintings by Böcklin,[93] namely 'Pietà', 'Splashing in the Waves', 'The Mood of Spring' and 'Nymph of the Fountain'. These were works which encouraged him to pursue ideas about painting because of course he wanted to gain an exhaustive understanding of the matter—just as had been the case with Richard Wagner where the starting point had been the debates already mentioned—so as to become thoroughly involved in this aspect of the arts, which he subsequently continued to do at Weimar.

It happened during this period that certain scholars, including the one speaking to you here, were invited to participate in preparing the great Weimar edition of Goethe's works.[94] Those commissioned by Grand-Duchess Sophie of Weimar[95] to distribute the various tasks were initially of the opinion that the person mentioned here should be allotted only Goethe's *Theory of Colour*. But later, after he had moved to Weimar to edit the *Theory of Colour*—and especially on account of his cordial friendship with Bernhard Suphan,[96] whose life was to end so tragically—Rudolf Steiner was allotted the editorship of all the scientific works. Thus began the period at Weimar when his work focused on natural science and philology. However, he has never been particularly self-satisfied with the philological side; he would be able to point out many a mistake in this connection and does not intend to gloss over the good many howlers he perpetrated.

After moving into the old Goethe-Schiller Archive[97]— which was still housed at the ducal residence—Rudolf Steiner also had other important experiences. Erudite individuals from Germany and abroad, even America, often visited the Archive which thus became a meeting place for all forms of scholarship. He was also able to observe the coming into being of a marvellously ideal institution, for this was the time when the new Goethe-Schiller Archive was being built on the other side of the river Ilm. He also had the unique opportunity to immerse himself in old reminiscences reaching back to the age of Goethe and Schiller. And since Weimar was a genuine meeting place for a variety of artistic endeavours—it was where Richard Strauss[98] began his career—Rudolf Steiner was also able to become familiar with those various endeavours.

After Rudolf Steiner had concluded his interpretation of the *Tale of the Green Snake and the Beautiful Lily*, the intensive work on Goethe came very much to the fore. Nevertheless, despite becoming immersed in Goethe, he also worked out his *Philosophy of Freedom*;[99] and he had already brought his paper on *Truth and Knowledge*[100] with him to Weimar. He still travelled to Vienna on a few occasions. Once he gave a lecture to the Goethe Society about the *Tale of the Green Snake and the Beautiful Lily*[101] and on another occasion he lectured to a scientific club about the relationship of monism to a more spiritual, more realistic orientation.[102] That was in 1893. The talk was printed in the monthly journal of the Science Club in Vienna. In it Rudolf Steiner dealt in depth with the relationship between philosophy and natural science. That lecture ended with a clear exposition of how he related to Ernst Haeckel with special emphasis on everything negative he had to say regarding him.[103]

It is now getting rather late, so it will not be possible to speak in the same detail, as has been the case thus far, about what followed. This is also not necessary. But if you were to investigate a great deal more of what occurred up to my time at Weimar—since the facts speak quite clearly for them- selves—you would find plenty of evidence to show what an incredible reversal of the truth is contained in the extra- ordinary claim—expressed yet again on a certain occasion by the President of the Theosophical Society[104]—that I was 'brought up by the Jesuits'. I have just been handed a copy of the *Stimmen aus Maria-Laach*,[105] which as we know is pub- lished by the Jesuits, containing the review of a book about theosophy; it contains a curious sentence. The book, by a Jesuit father, disapproves of theosophy. The review ends with the statement: 'The first part deals with the movement in general, its esotericism and false mysticism. The second part goes into detail, refuting the theosophical reveries about Christ ... The works to which the critic refers most fre- quently are *Christianity as Mystical Fact*[106] by Rudolf Steiner, (reportedly) an apostate priest and now General Secretary of the German Section of the Theosophical Society, and *Esoteric Christianity* by Mrs Besant, President of the Theosophical Society (headquarters in Adyar). Both books have already been translated into Italian.'[107]

It is thus stated even in the Jesuit journal *Stimmen aus Maria-Laach* that Rudolf Steiner is supposed to be 'an apostate priest'; so the Jesuits can pat themselves on the back for spreading this rumour. However, just as age is no excuse for folly, so Jesuitism protects no one against unjustly making objectively untrue assertions. And when a distortion of fact is spread in this way by Jesuits, surely Mrs Besant, of all people, should be suspicious. Yet she actually enlarges[108] on these things, so they circulate even further afield. Thus when I was in Graz recently[109] I had to counter these claims myself from the platform. It has also been alleged that I received a Jesuitical education at Kalksburg near Vienna.[110] I never saw the establishment at Kalksburg despite the fact that my relatives lived only three to four hours away from there. And as for a place called Bojkowitz,[111] the other location mentioned in this connection—well, I only even heard its name a few days ago.

All these details, which I feel it is really unreasonable to bother you with, will I am sure enable you to understand why I greatly resent having to waste so much time in refuting such rubbish. I have not made much of it so far, but when even the President of the Theosophical Society makes such claims there is nothing for it but to counter them with descriptions of how my education actually ran its course, namely in the form of a kind of self-schooling.

Everything I have told you—about the boy, the youth and the subsequent adult Rudolf Steiner—can be documented, and the facts will in every detail prove the utter foolishness and absurdity of the claims that are being made. There is no need for us to dwell on the moral aspect of this matter. What has been spoken of, and what still remains to be spoken of, are facts which can be checked at any time and which can be vouched for.

However, one might well ask from what right and based on what sources Mrs Besant can speak about my 'education as a young person' from which I have been 'insufficiently capable of extricating' myself, and from what right and based on what sources[112] her adherents—since they are unaware of the objections expressed here—will continue to make these claims. Some of them might even think of saying: But Mrs Besant is clairvoyant, so perhaps that is where she saw everything which she is now summarizing in her high-flown statement: 'He has been insufficiently capable of extricating himself from his education as a young person.'

It is better, therefore, to correct what derives from Mrs Besant's clairvoyance and indeed to examine that clairvoyance on the basis of such claims. The only way such clairvoyance can be tested is to put forward the facts. Now, at the starting point of our anthroposophical movement, it has been imperative for me to bore those who are standing by us at this starting point by presenting them with an alternative: either to examine the facts, every one of which can be verified, or else to accept the remarks made by Mrs Besant during the recent gathering of the Theosophical Society at Adyar—presumably, according to her adherents, on the basis of her clairvoyant visions.

*

Sources: This lecture was published in full for the first time in the 1946 *Nachrichtenblatt* (Dornach) having been edited by Marie Steiner on the basis of two longhand records based on shorthand reports. One of these is presumed to be by Walter Vegelahn; the author of the other is not known. The original shorthand reports are not extant. With a few minor editorial alterations, the 1946 version was also included in the book published in 1948 by Edwin Fröböse and Werner Teichert. The present publication has taken account of two further shorthand reports both of which are extant, one by Franz Seiler, the other by Berta Reebstein-Lehmann. This has led to the inclusion of several changes and additions. Michel Schweizer compared the two shorthand reports. The text as presented here was prepared by the editor with the inclusion of a few stylistic corrections.

Early Childhood 1861–68

An autobiographical fragment, undated

I was born on 25 February 1861[*] and baptized two days later at Kraljevec[113] on the border between Croatia and Hungary where my father served as a telegraphist on the Austrian Southern Railway. At that time the joint administration of the Southern Railway was still located in Vienna; the employees were moved around between the (later) Hungarian line and the Austrian lines. My father had been moved from a small railway station in Southern Styria to Kraljevec shortly before my birth.

My parents are both from the Horn area of Lower Austria.[114] My mother was born at Horn, my father at Geras in Lower Austria, the seat of a Premonstratensian establishment. In 1862 my father was moved from Kraljevec to Mödling near Vienna, and in 1863 to Pottschach.

My sister and brother[115] were born at Pottschach, and I spent my childhood there until my eighth year. The trains passing along the line, a nearby spinning mill, and the Austrian Schneeberg, together with the other Alpine mountains surrounding it, were everyday experiences for me. An estate with a castle owned by the Lichtenstein family was situated at Pottschach. The railway accountant's family visited us frequently. And the priest from the neighbouring village, St Valentin,[116] dropped in almost every day. This man conducted his life with no priestly pretentiousness; he was a man of the world. He called on us at the end of his daily walk and

---

[*] See Introduction regarding the date of birth.

was perhaps more interested in observing the passing and stopping trains than in any conversation with my parents. The Pottschach priest[117] also called on us frequently; he was not taken particularly seriously by his colleagues at St Valentin. The St Valentin priest was tall and the one from Pottschach was short, and I once witnessed a scene in which the former picked up the latter under his arm and bore him along for some distance like a parcel.

I soon became familiar with railway affairs because my favourite spots were the waiting room and my father's tiny office. I was sent to school at the age of six but was then removed because my father had fallen out with the teacher. When he became a pensioner I returned briefly to the Pottschach school under a young teacher. But mostly my father taught me himself.

The overall atmosphere was not conducive to developing any kind of sentimental effusiveness. The people with whom I came into contact were interested solely in the railway and the nearby spinning mill. The St Valentin priest was a steady individual, somewhat cynical in his conversation, and often quite droll.

The following experience made a profound impression on the boy.[118] My mother's sister had died tragically. She lived a good distance away from our village and my parents had not yet heard the news. Sitting in the station waiting room I witnessed the whole event. After I had hinted at this to my father and mother they only scolded me for being 'a foolish boy'. A few days later I saw my father looking serious after reading a letter he had received. Later I noticed my parents talking together and my mother in tears for several days. I was only told years later about the tragic event.

During that period all I learned was reading and arithmetic; I made no progress in writing.

When I reached my eighth year my father was transferred to Neudörfl near Wiener-Neustadt.[119] So then I attended school there. The teacher was horrified by my writing. I rounded off all the letters, ignored the upper portions and misspelled all the words. But among the teacher's books I discovered one of Močnik's geometry volumes.[120] I borrowed this for a while and read it avidly. And I always participated as a listener during the piano lessons my teacher gave in his room.

That teacher was an excellent man.[121] He was good at drawing and gave me drawing lessons even though what I really needed would have been spelling and writing lessons. His annual salary was only 54 florins plus meals provided by the head teacher. The latter came to the school very rarely because he was in charge of local parish business. We chil-

Neudörfl in the Burgenland

dren were of the opinion that our teacher was a 'proper' teacher, whereas the head teacher 'knew nothing about anything'.

In those days my parents were not religious. Even in earlier times, at Pottschach, my father used to say: 'Serving one's employer takes precedence over serving one's God,' thus excusing himself for never attending church since doing his work left no time for praying. Despite this I became an 'altar boy' at Neudörfl and a favourite of the priest who also liked my father very much despite his non-attendance at church.

That priest[122] was a strong character, a Magyar from the top of his head to the sole of his foot, and a churchman sharp as a knife. On occasion his sermons caused the pews in that small church to quake. I owe him a great deal, for he it was who, in my ninth year, introduced me to an understanding of the Copernican world view. He did this on the basis of very instructive drawings. He came to the school twice a week. All the children enjoyed his catechism and his Bible lessons because he was such a likeable person. As an 'altar boy' I served at mass, during afternoon services, during funerals and at Corpus Christi celebrations. These duties came to an abrupt end. Several 'altar boys', including myself, had turned up too late to officiate. All of us were to be caned at school. I had an absolutely irresistible aversion to this and always managed to avoid the issue, so that I was, in fact, never caned. Nevertheless, my father was so indignant at the very idea of 'his son' being caned that he said: 'That's enough of serving in church. You are not going to do it anymore.'

Curriculum Vitae (1861–91)

Enclosed with the doctorate application dated
6 August 1891

Vita

I, Rudolf Steiner, son of Johann Steiner who resides at Brunn am Gebirge in Lower Austria, official on the Austrian Southern Railway, was born at Kraljevec in Hungary on 27 February 1861.

Having completed the *Volksschule*, I entered the *Landes-Oberrealschule* at Wiener-Neustadt in 1871 where I passed the leaving examination with the mark 'Outstanding' in July 1879. Thereafter I entered the Technical University in Vienna where for eight semesters I studied: Mathematics, Physics, Theoretical Mechanics, Zoology, Mineralogy, Chemistry, Botany, Geology, History of Literature and State Law, passing the semester examinations with an average mark of 'Excellent' on the basis of which I received a grant of 300 Austrian florins for each of the four years. At Vienna University I also guest-attended the lectures by Professor Koenigsberger on Mathematics, and those by Professors Zimmermann, Vogt and Brentano on Philosophy. Studying mathematics and the sciences awoke my interest in philosophy. I have taken up philosophical writing. My achievements in what is now my main subject are demonstrated by my writing, several examples of which I enclose herewith. These have received expressions of approval from leading authorities. Moriz Carrière, Conrad Hermann, Max Koch, Schaarschmidt and *Das Literarische Centralblatt*, among others, have made very favourable comments in their critiques.[123]

On the strength of my written work I have been entrusted with the editorship of a part of Goethe's scientific writings for the Weimar Goethe Edition.

I have also worked as a private tutor.[124] The enclosed testimonial[125] states in addition that during my years as a student I also studied Greek and Latin to a level which enabled me to teach even advanced pupils at the *Gymnasium*.

Prellerstrasse 2, Weimar. Home of the Eunike family. Rudolf Steiner wrote his Philosophy of Freedom *on the ground floor. Today this house is a hotel ('Alt Weimar').*

In recent months I have been exclusively occupied with my present work.

Rudolf Steiner
Weimar, Junkerstrasse 12 (pro tem)

Curriculum Vitae (1861–92)

For the Goethe Archive's personnel records at Weimar 1892

Rudolf Steiner

Born at Kraljevec, Hungary, on 27 February 1861, Geras Jurisdiction, Lower Austria, attended the *Landes-Mittelschule* at Wiener-Neustadt and thereafter the philosophical lectures at the University of Vienna and the science, mechanics and mathematics lectures at the Technical University from 1879 to 1883. Doctoral thesis on 'The basic question of a theory of knowledge'. Thereafter engaged to work on Goethe's scientific writings for *Kürschners Deutsche National-Literatur*. Wrote *Goethe's Theory of Knowledge* (1886), *Goethe as the Founder of a New Science of Aesthetics* (1889), *Truth and Knowledge* (1892). From 24 July to 17 August 1889 and from 30 September 1890 until the present time he worked at the Goethe Archive on Goethe's morphological and geological works as well as his general scientific works.

During the winter of 1891–92, St. gave a lecture at the Goethe Archive, Vienna, on 'The enigma of Goethe's mysterious tale [in the emigrés[126]]' and two lectures at Weimar: 1. 'Imagination as a product of nature and a creator of culture'; 2. 'Weimar at the centre of German cultural life'.[127]

Submitted in November 1892

Twenty-four Questions to Rudolf Steiner and His Personal Replies

Motto: In God's place the free human being!!!

Your favourite characteristics in a man? *Energy.*
Your favourite characteristics in a woman? *Beauty.*
Your favourite occupation? *Pondering and musing.*
Your idea of happiness? *Pondering and musing.*
Which profession appears to you to be the best? *Whichever can annihilate you with the energy it generates.*
Who would you like to be if not yourself? *Friedrich Nietzsche before his madness.*
Where would you like to live? *I do not mind.*
When would you like to have lived? *In times when something needs to be done.*
Your idea of unhappiness? *Not knowing what to do.*
Your most characteristic trait? *I do not know.*
Your favourite writers? *Nietzsche, Hartmann, Hegel.*
Your favourite painters and sculptors? *Rauch, M. Angelo.*
Your favourite composers? *Beethoven.*
Your favourite colour and flower? *Violet, autumn crocus.*
Favourite historical heroes? *Attila—Napoleon, J. Caesar.*
Favourite historical heroines? *Catherine of Russia.*
Favourite characters in poetry? *Prometheus.*
Your favourite names? *Radegunde. Let the ladies decide.*
Which historical characters do you detest? *The weaklings.*
Which fault would you most readily forgive? *All of them once I have understood them.*
Your most extreme aversion? *Pedantry and a sense of order.*
Of what are you afraid? *Punctuality.*

Your favourite food and drink? *Frankfurter sausages and cognac. Black coffee.*

Your temperament? *Changeability.*

Weimar, 8 February [18]92   *Rudolf Steiner*

Transitions 1861–1906

An autobiographical sketch for Edouard Schuré at Barr, Alsace, September 1907

My attention was drawn to Kant very early on. In my fifteenth and sixteenth years I studied Kant very intensively, and before I transferred to University in Vienna I also intensively studied his generally accepted successors from the beginning of the nineteenth century who are entirely forgotten and scarcely ever mentioned by mainstream historians. Then I delved very thoroughly into Fichte and Schelling. This was the period—and it was connected with external esoteric influences—when I attained complete clarity concerning the concept of time. This realization had no connection with my studies and was directed entirely out of esoteric life. It was the realization that there exists a backward evolution which interacts with onward evolution—the esoteric-astral. This realization is a precondition for spiritual vision.[128]

Then came my acquaintance with the agent of t.M. [the Master[129]].

Then intensive study of Hegel.

Then the study of more recent philosophical thought which has been advancing in Germany since the [eighteen] fifties, specifically the so-called theory of knowledge in all its ramifications.

In my boyhood my life ran its course—without this being outwardly planned—in such a way that I never met anyone who presented me with a superstitious belief. Indeed, if any kind of superstition came to be mentioned by those around me it was *never* met by anything other than strongly emphatic rejection. I did become acquainted with church practices through participation in services as an altar-boy, but there was never any real piety or religiosity even among the priests whom I came to know. On the contrary, I frequently came across certain darker aspects of the Catholic clergy.

*

I did not immediately encounter the M. [Master], but met instead a person sent by him,[130] who was thoroughly initiated into the mysteries of how all plants have their effect and how they are connected with the cosmos and with the nature of the human being. Communication with the spirits of nature was something he took for granted and mentioned without any excitement, while the excitement it awakened in me was all the greater.

My official studies concerned mathematics, chemistry, physics, zoology, botany, mineralogy and geology, and these provided a far more secure basis for a spiritual view of the world than would have been the case with history or literature which had no significant prospects among the subjects to be studied in Germany at that time.

I became acquainted with Karl Julius Schröer[131] in Vienna during my early years at the university. Initially I attended his lectures on the history of German literature since Goethe's first appearance, on Goethe and Schiller, on the history of German literature in the nineteenth century, and on Goethe's *Faust*. I also participated in his tutorial course on 'Speaking in public and clarity in writing'. This was a remarkable university tutorial after the pattern of that established by Uhland at Tübingen University.[132]

Schröer came from the field of German philology; he had undertaken important studies of German dialects in Austria;

he was a researcher after the manner of the Brothers Grimm, and he admired the literary research of Gervinus. Prior to that he had been head teacher of the *Wiener Evangelische Schulen*. He is the son of the poet and most excellent pedagogue Christian Oeser. During the period of our acquaintance his studies were devoted entirely to Goethe. He has written a widely read commentary on Goethe's *Faust* and also on other dramas by Goethe. He studied at the universities of Leipzig, Halle and Berlin before the decline of German Idealism. He was a living embodiment of truly distinguished German scholarship. He was a captivating *human being*. We soon became friends and I was often invited to his home. It resembled an idealistic oasis within the arid materialism of German culture. External life at that time was filled with Austria's nationalistic struggles. Schröer distanced himself from the natural sciences.

From early 1880 onwards I was working on Goethe's scientific studies.

Then Joseph Kürschner[133] founded the comprehensive publication *Deutsche National-Literatur* for which Schröer edited Goethe's dramas, adding introductions and commentaries. On the recommendation of Schröer, Kürschner commissioned me to edit Goethe's scientific writings.

Schröer wrote an introduction through which he introduced me to the literary public.

Within this comprehensive work I wrote introductions to Goethe's botany, zoology, geology and the theory of colour.

Readers of these introductions will be able to detect theosophical ideas in them, clothed in the garment of a philosophical idealism. They will also find an appraisal of Haeckel. The theory of knowledge I developed in 1886 can be regarded as a philosophical supplement to this.

Through my acquaintance with the Austrian poetess M. E. delle Grazie,[134] who had found a fatherly friend in Professor Laurenz Müllner,[135] I was introduced into the circle of Viennese professors of theology. Marie Eugenie delle Grazie had written a great epic *Robespierre* and a drama *Schatten*.

Towards the end of the [eighteen] eighties I was briefly editor of the *Deutsche Wochenschrift*[136] in Vienna. This enabled me to concern myself in depth with the folk souls of the various Austrian nationalities. It was necessary to gain a coherent line within the politics of culture.

In all this it was out of the question to present ideas concerning esotericism in the public domain. The esoteric powers backing me gave me only a single piece of advice: 'Present everything in the garment of idealistic philosophy.'

Alongside all this I was also occupied for over 15 years with my work as an educator and private tutor.[137]

My first contact with theosophical circles in Vienna during the [eighteen] eighties had to remain *without* any external consequences.

During my final months in Vienna I wrote my small essay 'Goethe as the Founder of a New Science of Aesthetics'.

I was then called to the newly founded Goethe and Schiller Archive at Weimar in order to edit Goethe's scientific writings. My situation there was not official; I was merely a member of the team working on the *Sophienausgabe* or Weimar Edition of Goethe's works.

My next aim was to elaborate *purely philosophically* the basis of my view of the world. This was done in the two works *Truth and Knowledge* and *The Philosophy of Freedom*.

The Goethe and Schiller Archive was visited by numerous scholarly and literary, and also other, personalities from Germany and abroad. I became more closely acquainted with a good many of those personages because I was soon on friendly terms with the director of the Archive, Professor Bernhard Suphan,[138] and was frequently a guest at his house. Suphan invited me to participate in many private visits of guests at the Archive. It was on one of those occasions that I met Treitschke.

A more intimate friendship developed with the German researcher into myths and legends, Ludwig Laistner, author of *Rätsel der Sphinx*, who died soon afterwards.

I also had frequent conversations with Herman Grimm who spoke a great deal about a work which he never completed, a 'history of German imagination'.

Then came my *Nietzsche episode*. Shortly before this I had even written negatively about Nietzsche.[139]

My inner esoteric powers instructed me to allow the orientation towards the truly spiritual to flow unnoticed into the stream of time. One arrives at knowledge not by insisting exclusively on one's own point of view but by immersing oneself in other spiritual streams.

So I wrote my book about Nietzsche in that I placed myself firmly onto Nietzsche's point of view. Perhaps for this very reason it is the most objective book about Nietzsche written within Germany. Nietzsche comes into his own here as an anti-Wagnerian and an antichristian. For a while after this I was regarded as the most unequivocal 'Nietzschean'.

The 'Society for Ethical Culture' was founded in Germany at that time. This society was seeking a morality which was entirely independent of every world view. A complete phantasm and a threat to culture. I wrote a sharply critical article *against* that foundation in the weekly journal *Die Zukunft*.

Vehement protests ensued. And my prior occupation with

Nietzsche led to a pamphlet against me entitled: 'Nietzsche-Idiots'.[140]

The esoteric viewpoint calls for: 'No unnecessary polemics' and 'Wherever you can, avoid defending yourself'. I quietly finished writing my book *Goethe's World View* which brought my time at Weimar to a close.

Haeckel approached me immediately after the publication of my article in *Die Zukunft*. Two weeks later he wrote a piece for the same journal expressing agreement with my view that an ethic can only grow upon the soil of a world view.

Soon after that came Haeckel's sixtieth birthday which was celebrated with much festivity in Jena. Haeckel's friends included me in this. That was when I saw him for the first time. His personality is enchanting. In his person he is the complete opposite of the tone in his writings. If he had ever studied philosophy—in which he is not merely a dilettante but an infant—he would surely have drawn the loftiest spiritual conclusions from his epoch-making phylogenetic investigations.

Despite German philosophy as a whole, notwithstanding all the rest of German culture, Haeckel's phylogenetic ideas constitute the most significant deed of German cultural life in the second half of the nineteenth century. No better foundation for esotericism exists than Haeckel's doctrine. It is great, but Haeckel is its worst elucidator. It is not by demonstrating Haeckel's weaknesses to one's contemporaries that one does a service to cultural life; rather one should expound upon the greatness of his phylogenetic ideas. This is what I did in the two volumes of my *World and Life Conceptions in the Nineteenth Century*, which are dedicated to Haeckel, and also in my small book *Haeckel und seine Gegner*.

The age of German cultural life *is alive* solely in Haeckel's phylogeny. Philosophy itself is in a state of utter sterility; theology is a hypocritical web which is totally unaware of its own lack of truthfulness; and despite the great boom in empiricism, the sciences have fallen prey to the most desolate philosophical ignorance.

I was at Weimar from 1890 to 1897.

In 1897 I moved to Berlin as editor of the *Magazin für Literatur*. My books *World and Life Conceptions in the Nineteenth Century* and *Haeckel und seine Gegner* were written in Berlin.

My next task was to have consisted in bringing to expression a spiritual stream in literature. I placed the *Magazin* at the service of this task. It was a well-respected organ of long standing; it had been in existence since 1832 and had passed through various phases.

Gently and slowly I guided it towards an esoteric direction. I did this carefully yet clearly by writing an essay on 'Goethe's Secret Revelation and the Riddle of Faust' which simply reproduced what I had hinted at publicly in Vienna about Goethe's *Tale of the Green Snake and the Beautiful Lily*.

It came about quite naturally that a circle of readers gradually arose who were interested in the direction I had introduced into the *Magazin*. Financially, however, it did not develop as rapidly as the publisher would have wished. I wanted to provide a spiritual basis for the trend being followed by younger writers and was indeed in lively contact with its more promising followers. On the one hand I was left in the lurch, and on the other the trend soon collapsed into insignificance or else into naturalism.

Meanwhile my links with the workers' movement had begun to take shape. I had become a teacher at the Berlin Workers' Training School. I lectured on history and also the sciences. My thoroughly idealistic method for history and also the way I spoke soon came to be appreciated and understood by the working people. My audience increased and I was soon being asked to give talks every evening.

Then came the moment when, in agreement with the esoteric powers supporting me, I was able to say to myself: You have given your world view its philosophical basis, you have demonstrated a comprehension of current trends by dealing with them in a manner which is only possible for someone who fully understands them; no one will be justified in saying, 'This esotericist only speaks about the spiritual world because he is ignorant of the philosophical and scientific achievements of the time in which he lives.'

I had now also reached my fortieth year prior to which, according to the Masters,[141] no one may speak publicly as a teacher of esotericism. (It is a matter of error when an individual teaches at an earlier age.)

So I was able to turn publicly to theosophy. One consequence was that certain socialist leaders insisted on a general meeting of the Workers' Training School at which a choice was to be made between me and Marxism. But I was *not* ostracized. The general meeting decided with *all* votes except *four* to retain me as a lecturer.

Nevertheless, the 'terrorism' exerted by the leaders meant that I had to resign after three months. To avoid compromising themselves they used the pretext of claiming that I was too taken up with the theosophical movement and therefore had insufficient time for the Workers' Training School.

Fräulein von Sivers[142] was at my side almost from the beginning of my theosophical activity. She also witnessed the final phases of my relationship with the workers of Berlin.

★

Christian Rosenkreutz went to the Orient in the first half of the
fifteenth century in order to discover the balance between the
initiation of the East and that of the West.[143] One consequence of this was *the definitive* founding of the Rosicrucian
Movement in the West after his return. Rosicrucianism in
this form was to be the strictly secret school for the preparation of what was to become the public task of esotericism
around the turn of the nineteenth to the twentieth century
when external science was to have attained a preliminary
resolution to certain problems.

Christian Rosenkreutz named these problems as:

1) The discovery of spectral analysis by means of which the
physical constitution of the cosmos came to light.

2) The introduction of physical evolution into the science
of the organic realm.

3) Recognition of the fact of a form of consciousness dif-
fering from the ordinary through acceptance of hypnotism
and suggestion.

Not until *these* physical insights had matured within the
sciences were certain Rosicrucian principles to emerge from
esoteric science into the public domain.

Until then, Christian-mystical initiation was given in the
West in the form in which it flowed into St Victor, Meister
Eckhart, Tauler, etc. through what the Initiator gave to the
'Unknown Man from the High Lands'.[144]

The initiation of *Mani*[145]—who initiated Christian
Rosenkreutz in 1459—is regarded as a 'higher degree' within
this whole stream; it consists in the true recognition of the
function of evil. Together with what stands behind it, this

initiation must as yet remain concealed from the general public for a long time. Wherever even the smallest glimpse of it has entered into literature, the result has been calamitous, as happened through the noble Guyau whose pupil Friedrich Nietzsche became.

★

For your information: it cannot yet be expressed directly in this form.[146]

The Theosophical Society was founded in New York in 1875 by H.P. Blavatsky and H.S. Olcott. This initial foundation was decidedly western in character. The book *Isis Unveiled*, in which Blavatsky published very many esoteric truths, was similarly western in character. It has to be said about this book, however, that the great truths it communicates are frequently expressed in a distorted or indeed a caricatured fashion. It is like seeing a harmonious countenance in the distorted reflection of a convex mirror. The things which are said in *Isis* are true; but *how* they are said is a disorderly reflection of the truth. The reason for this is as follows. The truths themselves are *inspired* by the great *Initiates of the West* who were also the Initiators of the Rosicrucian wisdom; the distortion arose from the inappropriate manner in which the truths were assimilated by the *soul* of H.P. Blavatsky. To those who are knowledgeable in such matters, this is the *very fact* which should have provided proof of the higher source of inspiration from which these truths emanated. No one passing these truths on in such a distorted manner could have generated them *within him or herself*. Seeing how slender the opportunity is for them to bring the stream of spiritual wisdom into humanity in this way, the Initiators of the West decided to desist for the present from *this form* of communication. However, for better or worse, the door was now open: Blavatsky's soul was now conformable to the reception of spiritual wisdom. So the *eastern* Initiators were able to take possession of it. Initially these eastern Initiators had the best intentions. They saw how Anglo-Americanism was driving humanity towards the terrible danger of complete materialization of the imagination. They—these eastern Initiators—wanted to inoculate the western world with *their own* form of well-tried spiritual knowledge. It was under the influence of this stream that the Theosophical Society gained its eastern character; and the inspiration for Sinnett's *Esoteric Buddhism* and Blavatsky's *Secret Doctrine* came from the same source. Both works again became distortions of the truth. Sinnett's *Esoteric Buddhism* misrepresents the sacred announcements of the Initiators by an inadequate philosophical intellectualism, and Blavatsky's *Secret Doctrine* is distorted by her own chaotic soul.

The consequence of this was that the Initiators, including those from the East, increasingly withdrew their influence from the official Theosophical Society so that it became a playground for all kinds of esoteric powers which distort the lofty cause. A minor episode occurred during which Annie Besant entered into the stream of the Initiators through her pure and high-minded way of thinking and leading her life. But this small episode ended when she devoted herself to the influences of certain Indians who, under the sway chiefly of German philosophical dogmas which misinterpreted, developed a grotesque intellectualism. This was the situation when I became faced with the necessity of joining the Theosophical Society. Genuine Initiators had been present at its birth, and *therefore*, despite the fact that subsequent events have given it a degree of imperfection, it is *temporarily* an instrument for the spiritual life of the present time. Its successful development in western countries will depend entirely upon the degree to which it becomes capable of including Western Initiation within its sphere of influence. This is because Eastern Initiations must of necessity refrain from touching upon the *Christ Principle* as the central *cosmic* factor of evolution. Without this principle, however, the theosophical movement would have to remain without any determining effect on the western cultures which have the life of Christ as their starting point. The revelations of oriental initiation would have to take their place like a form of sectarianism *beside* the living culture. They could only hope for success in evolution if they were to eradicate the Christ Principle from western culture. This, though, would be the same as extinguishing the true *purpose of the earth*, which lies in the knowledge and realization of the intentions of the *living Christ*. It is the revelation of this in all its wisdom, beauty and purposefulness which is the most profound goal of Rosicrucianism. The only possible opinion regarding the value of eastern wisdom as an object of study is that this study is of the utmost value because western peoples have lost their understanding of esotericism whereas those in the East have retained it. Regarding the *introduction* of proper esotericism in the West only one opinion is possible, namely that it can only be the Rosicrucian-Christian path because *this* is the path which has been born out of life in the West and because its loss would cause mankind on earth to deny its purpose and its destiny. It is only within this esotericism that the harmony between science and religion can flourish. Any fusion of western science with eastern esotericism can only bring forth barren shams such as Sinnett's *Esoteric Buddhism*.

That which is correct can be depicted in a diagram:

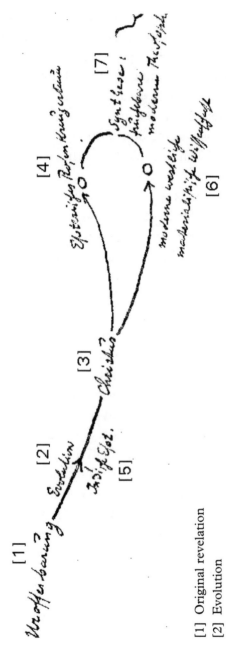

[1] Original revelation
[2] Evolution
[3] Christ
[4] Esoteric Rosicrucianism
[5] Indian esotericism
[6] Modern western materialistic science
[7] Synthesis: fruitful modern Theosophy

That which is incorrect, of which Sinnett's *Esoteric Buddhism* and Blavatsky's *Secret Doctrine* are examples:

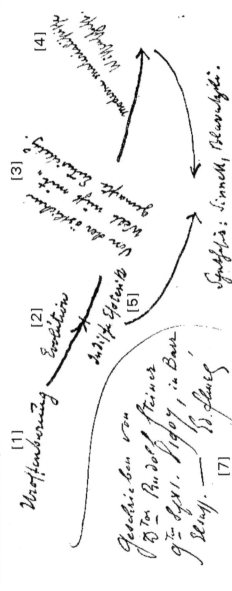

In R. Steiner's handwriting
[1] Original revelation
[2] Evolution
[3] Development not shared by the eastern world
[4] Modern materialistic science
[5] Indian esotericism
[6] Synthesis: Sinnett, Blavatsky

In E. Schuré's handwriting
[7] Written by Doctor Rudolf Steiner, 9th Sept,
1907, at Barr, Alsace—Ed. Schuré

From University Days to the Founding of the Anthroposophical Society 1879–1913

An autobiographical fragment, undated

Rudolf Steiner, b. 27 February 1861 at Kraljevec in Hungary; son of an official on the Austrian Southern Railway. The family came from the *Waldviertel* in Lower Austria and were of the peasant class. Initially studied science and mathematics at the Technical University, Vienna, while also turning to literary history and philosophy. Having been led thus to Goethe's scientific writings, he took these as the starting point for a thorough investigation of Goethe's world view. Encouraged in this and frequently assisted by Viennese Goethe scholar K.J. Schröer, who became a fatherly friend. These Goethe studies led in the [eighteen] eighties to St. editing Goethe's scientific writings with detailed introductions and commentaries for Kürschner's *Deutsche National-Literatur*. During this period it became necessary for him to establish a philosophical basis for Goethe's world view in his *Goethe's Conception of the World*. These Goethe publications led to his being invited to participate in work on the scientific writings for the Weimar Goethe Edition; he therefore lived at Weimar from 1890 to 1897. During this period he endeavoured, in his *Philosophy of Freedom* (1894), to set forth a systematic portrayal of his knowledge of the spiritual world arrived at through direct intuition. This book brought him into contact with Nietzsche, and this led to the publication of 'Nietzsche and his Opponents' (1895).[147] He presented the greater understanding of Goethe gained during his time at Weimar in *Goethe's World View* (1897).

From 1897 to 1900 he edited the *Magazin für Literatur*. In 1900 and 1901 he published *World- and Life-Conceptions in the Nineteenth Century* [which later appeared in summary and with additions under the title *The Riddles of Philosophy* in 1914]. He subsequently expanded on the seeds of a world view of intuition which had already been present in *Goethe's World View* and *The Philosophy of Freedom* (which seeks to attain spiritual experiences in the same way as experiences are achieved by means of the external senses) in his books: *Mysticism at the Dawn of the Modern Age* (1901); *Christianity as Mystical Fact* (1902); *Theosophy* (1904); and *Esoteric Science* (1909). He endeavoured to depict those seeds in sequences of pictures in *The Portal of Initiation* (1910); *Trials of the Soul* (1911); *The Guardian of the Threshold* (1912); and *The Souls' Awakening* (1913). Further descriptions of intuitive-spiritual observation methods may be found in *Knowledge of the Higher Worlds* (1910);[148] *A Road to Self-Knowledge* (1912); *The Threshold of the Spiritual World* (1913), and others.

In 1902 the affirmation of his view of the world by leading members of the Theosophical Society made it possible for St. outwardly to join that Society (which had its centre at Adyar); in this external affiliation with it he then set forth, also in numerous lectures and in the journal *Lucifer Gnosis*, the intuitive world view of spiritual science which he represented. The independent course he followed by comparison with that of the Theosophical Society led in 1913 to his exclusion from that Society together with all his adherents who then set about founding the independent 'Anthroposophical Society'.

[end of fragment]

A Vision (around 1884)

*An extract from the talk given at Kassel on 10 May
1914 in memory of Maria Strauch-Spettini*

Permit me to sketch a few pictures showing what will
increasingly be comprehended by the souls of human beings
once spiritual science has become a living factor within
human souls. When speaking of such things it is necessary to
take the concrete facts of spiritual research as one's point of
departure since with their help one can give graphic
descriptions which show how the individual relates and can
relate to the spiritual world.

I know a man[*] who, in his twenty-third or twenty-fourth
year, had a kind of vision. Initially he produced what was—
one might say—a rather inept written description[149] of that
vision in which the more important minds of German cultural life in the late eighteenth and early nineteenth century
were shown rather awkwardly as though in a kind of pageant.
He did not really know why he made that scenic portrayal:
what Goethe did, what Lessing, Schiller, Herder did when
removed into the world which human beings enter once they
have stepped through the portal of death. The person in
question had a vision of the life of such great geniuses up
above in the world of spirit, as though seeing what they were
doing there. From the point of view of spiritual research one
must ask oneself: What is the meaning of a vision like this?
What is it telling us?

Well, a vision like this represents a tremendous pene-

---

[*] See Introduction

tration of the spiritual world into the human soul. Specific influences from the spiritual world descend upon the soul, forcing their way into it and becoming something like a tremendous dream which impels one to express, but not clearly, what one feels and senses inwardly in the kind of vision I have suggested. Influences work upon the soul from out of the spiritual world. Yes, but how do these influences work? What is the relationship of the human soul to the beings of the spiritual world? For those who have died are also beings of the spiritual world during their time between death and a new birth. How does this relationship work?

Dear friends, when you look at an object in the physical world you are indeed seeing it—that is the correct way to describe this. I see a rose; I see the table. But it is not quite correct to use the same expression with reference to the beings of the spiritual world. It is not quite correct, not quite accurate to say: I see a being from among the ranks of the angels or the archangels. It is not correct to say this, for the situation is different.

As soon as we step into the spiritual world, feeling and experiencing ourselves there, we do not in fact look at the beings in it for it is they who look at us; we feel their spiritual senses and their spiritual forces as though resting upon our own soul, as though shining into our own soul and resounding there. Actually, what one should say about the spiritual world is: It is not I who am looking, not I who am perceiving, for I know that I am being looked at, I am being perceived.

You must sense this overall change which takes place within your inner experience when the words no longer mean what is said in the physical world: I perceive an object. Now, other words become meaningful: I myself, transported into the spiritual world, am being perceived from all sides; this is my life now. The 'I' knows about being perceived in this way, about the way in which the other beings embrace the experiences they have with me.

When this change takes place you then become aware of its significance for the soul in its whole relationship with its surroundings. You will become aware to some extent of how the soul has entirely different experiences when it ascends from the physical to the spiritual world. One part of the task to be performed by those who have died consists in their having to cast their glance, their spiritual glance, towards those still living on the earth, so that they, as it were, employ their forces in order to observe those living on the earth; the souls living on the earth are perceived by the souls of the dead. Through spiritual science people will learn to comprehend the meaning of the words: Those who have passed through the portal of death cast their glance upon me, they enliven me, they are with me, their forces shine down upon me.

People will learn to speak of the dead as living beings, beings living in spirit.

The person who experienced the vision just described found this relationship breaking through to him in a way which was unclear. In truth, Lessing, Goethe, Schiller, Herder are not inactive in the spiritual world after death; they concern themselves with those who are down below on the earth, they look upon them and perceive them, they enliven them in accordance with the forces they receive from the higher hierarchies. And so, without becoming consciously aware of it, the one who had that vision felt how he was being observed, as he stood upon the earth, by the spirits who are sent into human evolution. Such an experience can be unclear, and this had an impact upon the vision which he then clothed in inept words, describing how Lessing, like a marshal of the spiritual world, strode ahead followed by Goethe, Schiller, Herder, leading and guiding those who come later and still live on the earth.

A vision of this kind may be chaotically unclear and dreamlike, but when it appears before the soul in all clarity it can be significant for the person concerned. It can mean that he receives a conscience which is directly aroused by the spiritual world, so that he is able to strive, for example, towards the following thought: I will say what I say and do what I do in a way which enables me to endure the glance directed down towards me by those who have died. It may also be the case that, having awakened a vision such as the one described to full inner life, a person living here will feel that there is a task, small or large, which he must fulfil, and that his strength grows, that his courage and energy grow, that it becomes easier to satisfy his conscience by doing what is right if he says to himself: The dead are assisting me by turning their gaze upon me.

This is how the dead may become helpers for the living. What we learn through spiritual science is to feel responsible in what we are doing with regard to the dead. But we also come to experience the inspiring feeling which tells us that as we do one thing or another, one or other among those who have died is watching us with his active strength. His strength grows towards our strength.

It is not that the dead person gives us strength, for we must develop that ourselves; it is not that he gives us the talents, for we must possess these ourselves. He gives us veritable help, as though he were standing right behind us. And he is indeed standing right behind us.[150]

Notes

References to Rudolf Steiner's Collected Works in German, the *Gesamtausgabe*, are given thus: GA 23.

1. Kraljevec (Königsdorf), then in [Austro]-Hungary (now Croatia), was situated on the neck of land known as the 'Mura Island' formed by the confluence of the Mura and Drava rivers; beside the Bratislava–Pettau railway line.
2. Mödling, approx. 10 km south-west of Vienna on the Vienna–Baden–Wiener-Neustadt railway line.
3. Pottschach, on the Semmering Railway between Wiener-Neustadt and the Semmering Pass.
4. Johann Steiner (b. Geras 23 June 1829, d. Horn 22 January 1910); on 16 May 1860 m. Franziska, née Blie (b. Horn 8 May 1834, d. Horn 24 December 1918). Both villages are located in the so-called 'Waldviertel' district of Lower Austria. See also Note 82 on 'Bandlkramerlandl'.
5. The Semmering Railway, built 1848–54, was Europe's first great mountain railway.
6. Vienna's fresh water supply was carried by an aqueduct from the Schneeberg region to Vienna.
7. The priest at Pottschach was called Ignatz Artner.
8. Leopoldine (b. Pottschach 1864, d. Horn 1927) and Gustav (b. Pottschach 1866, d. Scheibbs/Lower Austria 1942).
9. Fr. Robert Andersky, Cistercian Order, priest at St Valentin.
10. Neudörfl [literally: New Little Village] was founded in 1641. The name arose because of an objection by the inhabitants of Wiener-Neustadt [literally: Vienna New Town] to the 'new little village' on their doorstep.
11. 'Staberl' was a fictional Viennese buffoon character who always got into trouble through ignorance of local mores but then knew how to turn the situation to his advantage. The

author was Adolf Bäuerle (1784–1859). To date the picture book mentioned has not been identified.

12. This encounter with the deceased family member is presumed to have taken place during the final year (1868) at Pottschach. It is thought that the impressions of nature linked with it may be mirrored in the fairy tale 'The Miracle of the Spring' told in *The Soul's Probation*, the second of Rudolf Steiner's Mystery Dramas (GA 14).

13. Heinrich Gangl, assistant teacher.

14. Count Istvan Széchenyi (b. Vienna 1792, d. Döbling near Vienna 1860) was a Hungarian reformer and patriot known as 'the greatest of the Magyars' who was correspondingly admired by all and sundry. The charcoal drawing mentioned still exists in the Rudolf Steiner Archive at Dornach. A small reproduction may be found in *Beiträge zur Rudolf Steiner Gesamtausgabe, Booklet 83/84*, Dornach 1984, p. 41.

15. Franz Maráz, from 1860 to 1873 priest at Neudörfl and subsequently a canon at Ödenburg where he held a high office.

16. The misunderstanding mentioned here arose from what Edouard Schuré wrote in his foreword to Rudolf Steiner's book *Christianity as Mystical Fact* (Paris 1908). In the bibliographical details about Steiner he had stated, rather extravagantly: 'La poésie du culte, la profondeur des symboles l'attirait mysterieusement ...' This remark, that as a choir boy Rudolf Steiner had 'received profound mystical impressions while serving at the altar', was soon quoted by critics as proof of his supposed Jesuitical up-bringing. See Hans Freimark, *Geheimlehre und Geheimwissenschaft*, Leipzig 1913, pp. 84ff.

17. The Lodge of the Neudörfl Freemasons had been inaugurated in 1871. See 'Einweihung der Loge Humanitas in Neudörfl' in *Hajnal*, 1871/72, pp. 273ff.

18. Franz Močnik, Knight, b. Kirchheim/Görz 1814, wrote a

number of geometry textbooks. This may be a reference to *Lehrbuch der Geometrie*, with 265 woodcuts within the text, Vienna 1856; *Anfangsgründe der Geometrie in Verbindung mit dem Zeichnen. Für Unterrealschulen*, with 223 woodcuts within the text, 12th edition, revised, Prague 1867.

19. From the 1872/73 school year Rudolf Steiner attended the district *Ober-Realschule* in Wiener-Neustadt, an important industrial centre. He was permitted to attend this school because 'at the express request of his father he had been subjected to an examination to establish the level of his knowledge'. The examination took place at the *Volks-Bürger-Schule* in Wiener-Neustadt and showed the mark 'Very Good' in every subject. The subjects Singing and Physical Education were not tested. The certificate is dated 28 September 1872.

20. Rudolf Steiner's sister, Leopoldine, often went out to meet her brother in order, as she herself said, to help him carry his heavy bag of books and also, at first, to 'stand by him on account of their fear of gypsies'. See 'Aus der Schulzeit Rudolf Steiners' in C.S. Picht *Gesammelte Aufsätze, Briefe und Fragmente*, Stuttgart 1964, p. 38.

21. This good woman was Frau Lackinger whose husband was the chief bookkeeper at the locomotive factory.

22. Heinrich Schramm, regional director and inspector of schools from 1868 to 1874, was also headmaster of the *Ober-Realschule* in Wiener-Neustadt where he had taught mathematics since 1864. In the school's 'Eighth Annual Report' (1873) he published a thesis entitled 'The force of attraction as an effect of movement'.

23. Laurenz Jelinek was Rudolf Steiner's mathematics and physics teacher from the third class. At the end of the 1873/74 school year, a thesis on probability appeared in the school's 'Ninth Annual Report': 'The Cubic Numbers'

24. From the second class onwards, Georg Kosak (b. Vienna

1836, d. Graz 1914) was Rudolf Steiner's teacher for projective geometry and geometrical drawing. He was a man of many parts and also knowledgeable about art. The school's 'Twelfth Annual Report' contains his essay on 'The Constant Quotient in Geometry'. This teacher later moved to Graz. When Rudolf Steiner visited that town after almost 30 years of lecturing he tried in vain to contact Kosak. See the Breslau lecture of 11 June 1924 in *Karmic Relationships* (English Vol. VII, p. 71, German Vol. V, GA 239).

25. Heinrich Borchert Lübsen (b. Eckwarden, Oldenburg 1801, d. Altona 1864), *Einleitung in die Infinitesimal-Rechnung (Differential- und Integral-Rechnung) zum Selbstunterricht,* Hamburg 1855, 5th edition, Leipzig 1874, and many other books.

26. Balus, from Sauerbrunn near Neudörfl.

27. *Allgemeiner Mass- und Gewichtskalender, Ausführliche Umwandlungs-Tabellen sämtlicher in Österreich-Ungarn gebräuchlichen und neuen Masse und Gewichte. Bearbeitet und Zusammengestellt von einem Fachmann,* Vienna 1874.

28. Carl Hickel, M.D. (1813–1905), general practitioner and physician to the railway. He lived in Wiener-Neustadt at the corner of Frauengasse which leads into the Pfarrplatz. He wrote a letter to Rudolf Steiner on 6 January 1893 when he was already seriously ill and almost blind (see *Beiträge zur Rudolf Steiner Gesamtausgabe, Booklet 49/50,* Dornach 1975).

29. This subject, taught initially by Edward Grossmann and subsequently by Georg Kosak, was 'Geometry and Drawing' from the first to the fourth class and 'Projective Geometry and Drawing' from the fifth to the seventh class. In addition to these there was a subject known as 'Freehand Drawing' which began in the second class. Throughout the boy's schooling this was taught by Ferdinand Schuberth.

30. The small volumes of Reclam's *Universal-Bibliothek* began to appear in 1867 with Kant's works coming out in the mid-

1870s. Among these were *Zum ewigen Frieden. Ein philoso-phischer Versuch*; *Critique of Judgement*; *Critique of Practical Reason*; *Critique of Pure Reason* (May 1877, Rudolf Steiner was 16 years old; source Christoph Lindenberg, *Rudolf Steiner. Eine Chronik*, Stuttgart 1988, p. 46); *Von der Macht des Gemüts, durch den blossen Vorsatz seiner krankhaften Gefühle Meister zu sein*; *Religion Within the Bounds of Mere Reason*; *The Conflict of the Faculties*; *Dreams of a Spirit-Seer*.

31. In July 1879. For more detail see Note 37.

32. Hugo von Gilm (b. Innsbruck 1831, d. Wiener-Neustadt 1906) was Rudolf Steiner's chemistry teacher at the *Realschule* from the fourth to the seventh class. He was a half-brother of the poet Hermann von Gilm.

33. Hermann von Gilm (b. Innsbruck 1812, d. Linz 1864), lyricist with a liberal-minded view of politics and religion and an enthusiastic love of the Tyrol, his homeland. His 'Jesuit-enlieder' are also significant.

34. Henri Charles Ferdinand Marie Dieudonné d'Artois, Duke of Bordeaux, Count of Chambord (b. Paris 1820, d. Schloss Frohsdorf near Wiener-Neustadt 1883). Two attempts by the Legitimist Party to put him on the French throne as Henry V failed. Thereafter he lived as a landed aristocrat on his various estates, a man of honest clerical and absolutist views.

35. Gustav Lindner (b. Rozdalowitz, Bohemia 1828, d. Prague 1887), *Lehrbuch der empirischen Psychologie*, Vienna 1858, and *Einleitung in das Studium der Philosophie*, Vienna 1866.

36. Johann Friedrich Herbart (b. Oldenburg 1776, d. Göttingen 1841), philosopher. See also Note 50.

37. The *Maturitäts-Zeugnis* (final school certificate) from the *Ober-Realschule* of Wiener-Neustadt is dated 5 July 1879. The text ends as follows: 'It is hereby certified that the examinee has fulfilled the legal requirements with distinction. This certificate therefore qualifies him for attendance at a technical university.' The certificate bears the signature, among others,

of Councillor Eduard Walser, Area School Inspector, who, in 1884, drew the attention of the Specht family to Rudolf Steiner with regard to the position of tutor for their sons. See the letter from Pauline Specht to Rudolf Steiner dated 16 June 1884, in Rudolf Steiner, *Briefe, Band I, 1881–90,* No. 62 (GA 38): 'Having received a cordial recommendation from Councillor Dr Walser, I write to ask whether you might feel inclined to take up the position of tutor in my house.'

38. Karl von Rotteck (b. Freiburg 1775, d. Freiburg 1840), *Allgemeine Weltgeschichte,* nine volumes, Freiburg 1812–27. Numerous further editions.

39. At that time, religious instruction was only compulsory up to the fourth class of the *Ober-Realschule.* The boy's report shows the mark 'Satisfactory' at the end of the first six months; by the end of the fourth class he was awarded 'Excellent'.

40. Inzersdorf, to the south of Vienna on the Vienna–Münchendorf–Pottendorf–Wiener-Neustadt railway line. Rudolf Steiner lived here from the autumn of 1879 until 20 June 1882.

41. Karl Leonhard Reinhold (b. Vienna 1758, d. Kiel 1823), philosopher.

42. Wilhelm Traugott Krug (b. Radis near Gräfenhainichen 1770, d. Leipzig 1842), *Fundamentalphilosophie,* Züllichau 1803, 3rd Edition Leipzig 1827. The fundamental tenet of his philosophical system is described as 'transcendental syntheticism'.

43. Rudolf Steiner's matriculation date at the Technical University of Vienna was 3 October 1879. As the son of a railway official he was entitled to an annual grant of 300 florins established by Karl, Knight of Ghega, the builder of the Semmering Railway. Certificates confirming the successful completion of examinations are extant for the academic years 1879–82. The fourth year, 1882–83, is certified only by a list

of the courses attended. That Steiner intended to sit the fourth-year examinations is confirmed in an undated letter to his friend Albert Löger. See Rudolf Steiner, *Briefe, Band I, 1881–1890*, No. 13 (GA 38).

44. Karl Julius Schröer (b. Bratislava 1825, d. Vienna 1900), pedagogue, language and Goethe scholar, was Rudolf Steiner's fatherly friend and intellectual mentor during the 1880s. He had been Professor for Literature at the Technical University since 1867. The University's 'Commemorative Document' (1915) recounts his activities there. 'He lectured not only on the history of German literature in general and that of the nineteenth century in particular but also on outstanding poets such as Walther von der Vogelweide, Goethe and Schiller. He spoke on German grammar as a science and an educational subject, on the German classics and the German stage. And, under the auspices of the "German Society" he had founded, he instituted a kind of seminar for the practice of public speaking and descriptive writing which had been expected of students since 1870/72. Thus Schröer's teaching was extensive and included questions of public address with which technical scientists were on the whole not so familiar.'

Rudolf Steiner gave a comprehensive description of Karl Julius Schröer in *The Riddle of Man. From the Thinking Observations and Contemplations of a Series of German and Austrian Personalities: What They Have Said and Left Unsaid*, Mercury Press, Spring Valley 1990 (GA 20).

45. Felix Koguzki (b. Vienna 1833, d. Trumau 1909). His extant diary contains the following entry: 'Herr Steiner jun., student, resident at Inzersdorf, called on me on Sunday, 21 August 1881; unfortunately I was not at home. Herr St. came again on Friday, 26 inst.' See also Emil Bock, *The Life and Times of Rudolf Steiner, Vol. 1: People and Places*, Floris Books, Edinburgh 2008. See also Note 130.

46. This person remains unknown. Rudolf Steiner only once mentioned him as being a 'very significant personage' (see Friedrich Rittelmeyer, *Rudolf Steiner Enters My Life*, Christian Community Press, London 1963). See also Rudolf Steiner's notes for Edouard Schuré (p. 74–5 in the present volume) and his letter to Friedrich Eckstein at the end of November 1890 in Rudolf Steiner, *Briefe*, Vol. II (GA 39).

47. *An Outline of Esoteric Science*, Anthroposophic Press, Hudson 1997 (GA 13), initially published in English as *Occult Science, an Outline*.

48. As yet not identified. See also the book reference in Note 45.

49. On the importance of recognizing the significance of timing in Rudolf Steiner's spiritual research, see Hella Wiesberger: 'Rudolf Steiner's life's work is in its reality his life's course. The three years 1879–1882 as the true birth period of anthroposophical spiritual science', in *Beiträge zur Rudolf Steiner Gesamtausgabe, Booklet 49/50*, Dornach 1975.

50. Johann Friedrich Herbart *Allgemeine Metaphysik*, 2 volumes, Königsberg 1828/29. (See Note 36.)

51. Robert Zimmermann (b. Prague 1824, d. Vienna 1898), aesthetics scholar and philosopher; 1861–95 professor of philosophy at Vienna University. One of the most important proponents of the Herbart school.

52. Ottokar Lorenz (b. Iglau 1832, d. Jena 1904), 1860–1885 professor of history at Vienna University, and from 1885 at Jena.

53. Franz Brentano (b. Marienberg near Boppard 1838, d. Zurich 1917), philosopher, a nephew of Clemens Brentano, until 1873 a Catholic theologian, thereafter professor of philosophy at Würzburg until 1895.

54. This lecture by Ottokar Lorenz, 'Goethe's political apprenticeship' (published in Berlin), took place in 1893 during the Eighth General Assembly of the Goethe Society at Weimar. It dealt in detail with Goethe's dependence on Charles

Augustus (Karl August) in matters of policy and with his activity on behalf of the League of German Princes. See *Goethe-Jahrbuch*, Vol. XV, Frankfurt 1894.

55. Edmund Reitlinger (b. Pest 1830, d. Vienna 1882), was professor of physics at the Technical University from 1866. The book *Johannes Kepler* by Reitlinger, Neumann and Grüner was published in Stuttgart in 1868.

56. Moriz Zitter, d. Vienna 1921. At Hermannstadt (Sibiu) he published the *Deutsche Lesehalle für alle Stände* in which Rudolf Steiner's essay 'An independent view of the present day' (1884) appeared (in GA 30). In 1899, Zitter collaborated with Rudolf Steiner and O.E. Hartleben in publishing the *Magazin für Literatur*, Berlin.

57. *Arthur Schopenhauers sämtliche Werke in zwölf Bänden. Mit Einleitung von Dr. Rudolf Steiner*, J.G. Cottasche Buchhandlung Nachfolger, Stuttgart 1894. The introduction (Schopenhauer's Biography) is included in Rudolf Steiner *Biographien und biographische Skizzen 1894–1905* (GA 33).

58. *Deutsche Lesehalle* (until 1881 *Lese- und Redehalle der Technischen Hochschule in Wien*), originally part of the *Literarische Studentenvereine der Wiener Hochschulen*. This society played a leading role in some of the university's affairs, for instance those of the university's technical staff.

59. Johannes Volkelt (b. Lipnik/Galicia 1848, d. Leipzig 1930), *Erfahrung und Denken. Kritische Grundlegung der Erkenntnistheorie*, Hamburg 1886.

60. Richard Falckenberg (b. Magdeburg 1851, d. Jena 1920), philosopher.

61. Hermann Helmholtz (b. Potsdam 1821, d. Charlottenburg 1894), scientist.

62. Kuno Fischer (b. Sandelwalde 1824, d. Heidelberg 1907), *Geschichte der neueren Philosophie*, 10 volumes, Heidelberg 1897–1903.

63. Baron Lazar von Hellenbach (b. Castle Paczolay, Hungary

1827, d. Castle Paczolay 1887), philosopher and political scientist. In a public lecture given in Berlin on 30 May 1904 (in GA 52), Rudolf Steiner described him as 'a personage who remains insufficiently appreciated to this day'.

64. The essays 'Thomas Seebeck and Goethe's Theory of Colour' and 'One hundred years ago. On the Theory of Colour' were published in the Chronicle of the Vienna Goethe Society, ed. Karl Julius Schröer, Vienna 1886 (1st Year, Vol. 1), and 1887 (2nd Year, Vol. 7) in GA 30.

65. Joseph Kürschner (b. Gotha 1853, d. 1902 while travelling in the Tyrol), writer. Lived in Stuttgart 1881–92. Published *Deutsche National-Literatur* 1883–1901. This comprised 163 volumes and, alternatively, 221 volumes and an index volume. Of these, Volumes 82–117 covered the works of Goethe; therein XXXIII–XXXVI, 1st and 2nd part: Scientific Writings edited (with introductions and comments within the text) by Rudolf Steiner. The first two volumes came out in the W. Spemann Verlag, Berlin and Stuttgart. This then joined with Adolf Kröner (owner of the Cotta Verlag and other publishing houses) to form the 'Union Deutsche Verlagsgesellschaft, Stuttgart' which published the remaining volumes. After the first edition there was a reprint at Dornach in 1982. There is a separate edition of the 'Introductions' in GA 1. Correspondence between Karl Julius Schröer, Joseph Kürschner and Rudolf Steiner concerning the publication of Goethe's scientific writings (1882–84) is published in Rudolf Steiner, *Briefe, Band I (1881–1890)* (GA 38).

66. Rudolf Steiner, *A Theory of Knowledge Implicit in Goethe's World Conception*, Anthroposophic Press, New York 1978 (GA 2).

67. The bibliography *Das literarische Lebenswerk Rudolf Steiners*, Dornach 1926, compiled by Carlo Septimus Picht, includes the following essays for the years 1882/83: 'Goethe und

Shakespeare, eine Parallele', 'Über Hermann Hettner', 'Auf der Höhe', 'Lessing' all in the journal *Freie Schlesische Presse,* Troppau. Published by Der Deutsche Verein in Troppau, responsible editor: E. Pfeifer, D.Phil. (whose colleague was Emil Schönach, a friend of Steiner's in his younger days). Originals of these essays have so far not been found and there are no known copies. Picht comments: 'Since neither the Gymnasial-Museums-Bibliothek in Troppau nor the National-Bibliothek in Vienna (which should have received deposit copies), nor the publisher Strasilla in Troppau have possession of the early annual editions of the *Freie Schlesische Presse,* and since thorough personal investigations in Troppau and surroundings (with the kindest assistance of the poet Maria Stona, Castle Trzebowitz near Groppau, as well as of the editorship of the *Sudeten-Rundschau,* Troppau) have remained without result, there is nothing for it but to regard these important early publications as lost!' Further searches undertaken more recently have thus far also been unsuccessful. See also *Beiträge zur Rudolf Steiner Gesamtausgabe, Booklet 12,* 1964 and *Booklet 49/50,* 1975; also Edwin Fröböse on comments by Rudolf Steiner on the above-mentioned essays in *Booklet 51/52,* 1975, letters from Emil Schönaich to Rudolf Steiner.

68. 'Auf der Höhe' is the title of a work by Bertold Auerbach. Rudolf Steiner quoted Auerbach in the lecture he gave on 20 December 1889 at Hermannstadt, Siebenbürgen (now Sibiu, Transylvania), 'Die Frau im Lichte der Goetheschen Weltanschauung', now in *Beiträge zur Rudolf Steiner Gesamtausgabe, Booklet 61/62,* Dornach 1978.

69. Hermann Hettner (b. Leisersdorf 1821, d. Dresden 1882), literary and art historian and a friend of Gottfried Keller. Works: *Das moderne Drama* 1852; *Literaturgeschichte des 18. Jahrhunderts,* 3 volumes, 1856–70; *Griechische Reiseskizzen* 1853; *Italienische Studien* 1879.

70. The 1889 register of members of the Vienna Goethe Society includes Rudolf Steiner, Vienna IX, Kolin-Gasse 5. And in the 'Chronicle of the Vienna Goethe Society' of 1893 he is listed as a member of the committee.

71. This lecture took place on 9 November 1888 and was published in 1889 as an offprint from *Deutsche Worte*, Vienna (GA 30 and GA 271). In English: *Goethe as the Founder of a New Science of Aesthetics*, Anthroposophical Publishing Co., London 1922.

72. Upon the recommendation of Dr Eduard Walser, headmaster of the *Realschule* in Vienna, Rudolf Steiner worked from 10 July 1884 to 28 September 1890 in the house of Ladislaus (1834–1905) and Pauline (1846–1916) Specht, a Jewish merchant family in Vienna, as tutor to their four sons Richard, Arthur, Otto and Ernst. Their family doctor was the famous Viennese specialist in internal diseases, Josef Breuer, who is regarded as a pioneer of psychoanalysis. See Walter Kugler's documentation 'Rudolf Steiner als Hauslehrer und Erzieher, Wien 1884–1890' in *Beiträge zur Rudolf Steiner Gesamtausgabe, Booklet 112/113*, Dornach 1994.

73. Kalksburg, south-west of Vienna, was home to a Jesuit monastery.

74. In 1912 it was rumoured in Munich that in earlier years Rudolf Steiner had been seen at the Jesuit establishment at Bojkowitz in Moravia.

75. Marie Eugenie delle Grazie (b. Weisskirchen, Hungary 1864, d. Vienna 1931), poet living in Vienna from 1872.

76. Laurenz Müllner (b. Gross-Grillowitz, Moravia 1848, d. Merano 1911), Professor of Philosophy in Vienna, from 1894 chancellor of Vienna University. Rudolf Steiner frequently mentioned the lecture the Professor had given at his inauguration, 'The Significance of Galileo for Philosophy'. See Steiner's statements about Müllner in *The Riddle of Man* (1916) (GA 20).

77. Wilhelm Neumann, Cistercian Order (b. Vienna 1837, d. Mödling near Vienna 1919), one of the Catholic Church's must important scholars. On Neumann see also Rudolf Steiner, *The Philosophy of Thomas Aquinas*, 3rd lecture (GA 74).

78. Joseph Kopallik (b. Vienna 1849, d. by drowning near Fiume 1897), from 1886 Professor at Vienna University.

79. Heinrich Friedjung (b. Rostschin, Moravia 1851, d. Vienna 1920), historian and political writer. He founded the journal *Deutsche Wochenschrift* which appeared weekly from 4 November 1883. It described itself as 'an organ for the mutual national interests of Austria and Germany'. Dr Joseph Eugen Russell was co-editor, and after Friedjung's departure he continued publishing the journal until 1888. Rudolf Steiner joined the editorial staff at the beginning of 1888 through Russell. During the first six months he wrote the political leading articles (in *Gesammelte Aufsätze zur Kultur- und Zeitgeschichte 1887–1901*, GA 31). The publication ceased at the beginning of July 1888 through the fault of Russell.

80. Alexander Prince of Battenberg (b. Verona 1857, d. Graz 1893), chosen in 1879 by Tsar Alexander II, his uncle, to be Alexander I, Prince of Bulgaria. He abdicated in 1886 after being harshly rejected by Tsar Alexander III. Thenceforth he was known as a Count of Hartenau. In 1887—after a brief interregnum—Ferdinand of Koburg was installed as Ferdinand I, Prince of Bulgaria. The so-called Battenberg Affair also took place during 1888. The tension between Germany and Russia caused by Alexander of Bulgaria's courtship of Princess Victoria of Prussia was resolved through Bismarck's intervention. See also *Gesammelte Aufsätze zur Kultur-und Zeitgeschichte 1887–1901* (GA 31).

81. Robert Hamerling (b. Kirchberg am Wald, Lower Austria 1830, d. Graz 1889), 1851–66 teacher in Vienna, Graz, Cilli

and Trieste. Thereafter a writer of poetry. *Homunkulus. Modernes Epos in zehn Gesängen*, Hamburg 1888. On Hamerling, see also *Gesammelte Aufsätze zur Literatur 1884– 1902* (GA 32); *The Riddle of Man*, Mercury Press, New York 1990 (GA 20), and the lecture 'Robert Hamerling: Poet and Thinker' in *The Presence of the Dead*, Anthroposophic Press, New York 1990 (GA 154).

82. 'Bandlkramerlandl' ['district of the ribbon pedlars'], generally known as the 'Waldviertel' or 'Forest Quarter', it was once described by Hamerling as follows: 'I do not know whether the building of a railway which bordered upon the "Waldviertel" brought any change in its seclusion from the world. In 1867 the arrival of a stranger there was still an event. If someone came along on foot or in a cart, the ploughing cattle stopped in their tracks to gape sideways at the new apparition. The peasant made a few half-hearted attempts with his whip to get them moving again, but failed and so ended up doing as his animals did; the plough rested until the stranger disappeared behind the next hill or copse. This, too, is a picture displaying an idyllic mood.' From *Prosa, Skizzen, Gedenkblätter und Studien*, Hamburg 1884, Volume Two.

83. *Die Atomistik des Willens. Beiträge zur Kritik der modernen Erkenntnis*, 2 volumes, Hamburg 1891. Regarding the passage mentioned by Rudolf Steiner, see Volume I, the chapter on 'Analyse und Synthese', p. 63.

84. Of this correspondence, only two of Hamerling's letters are extant (30 January 1887 and 11 May 1888, both from Graz).

85. Rudolf Steiner was awarded his doctorate at the University of Rostock on 26 October 1891 (having taken the viva voce examination on 23 October). His dissertation was entitled 'The basic question of a theory of knowledge with especial reference to Fichte's doctrine of science. Prolegomenon regarding a philosophizing consciousness of self.' This was

published in book form in Weimar in 1892 with the addition of an introduction and one new chapter under the title *Truth and Knowledge, an Introduction to 'Philosophy of Spiritual Activity'*, Steinerbooks, New York 1981 (GA 3). See also the documentation edited by D. Hoffmann, W. Kugler and U. Trapp: 'Rudolf Steiners Dissertation. Mit textkritischen Anmerkungen, Rezensionen und zahlreichen unveröffentlichten Briefen und Dokumenten zum Lebensgang Rudolf Steiners' in the series *Rudolf Steiner Studien*, Vol. V, Dornach 1991.

86. Heinrich von Ferstel (b. Vienna 1828, d. Grinzing near Vienna 1883), Professor of Architecture at the Technical University in Vienna, built the Votive Church during the years 1865–79. Friedrich von Schmidt (b. Frickenhofen, Württemberg 1825, d. Vienna 1891), Professor at the Vienna Academy of Art, built the Town Hall between 1872 and 1883. Theophil von Hansen (b. Copenhagen 1813, d. Vienna 1891), Professor at the Vienna Academy of Art, completed the Austrian Parliament House in 1883, construction of which had commenced in 1874.

87. See Rudolf Steiner's 1906 lectures on Richard Wagner's musical dramas in *Die Welträtsel und die Anthroposophie* (GA 54). Also the lecture given in Nuremberg on 2 December 1907 in *Supersensible Knowledge*, Anthroposophic Press, New York and Rudolf Steiner Press, Bristol 1987 (GA 55).

88. Helena Petrovna Blavatsky (b. Ekaterinoslav, southern Russia 1831, d. London 1891). The Theosophical Society was founded by H.P. Blavatsky together with Colonel Henry Steel Olcott (1832–1907) in New York on 17 November 1875. Soon after this she moved her centre to India. See also *The Anthroposophic Movement*, 8 lectures, Rudolf Steiner Press, Bristol (GA 258).

89. Alfred Percy Sinnett, *Esoteric Buddhism*, Theosophical Publishing Society, London 1903.

90. Mabel Collins, *Light on the Path*, Theosophical Publishing House, London 1872.

91. Franz Hartmann (b. Donauwörth 1838, d. Kempten 1912), physician and theosophist, founded a section of his own within the Theosophical Society.

92. Rosa Mayreder (b. Vienna 1858, d. Vienna 1938), writer, a leader in the Austrian women's rights movement. See *Zur Kritik der Weiblichkeit*, Jena and Leipzig 1905.

93. It is presumed that the exhibition mentioned was that of October 1887 presented by the Austrian Society for the Arts in honour of Arnold Böcklin's 60th birthday; the paintings mentioned were on show there.

94. The so-called *Sophienausgabe* or Weimar Edition of Goethe's works was commissioned by Grand-Duchess Sophie of Weimar. From 1890 to 1896 Rudolf Steiner edited Volumes VI to XII of Section II, Scientific Writings.

95. Grand-Duchess Sophie Luise of Saxe-Weimar, Princess of the Netherlands (b. The Hague 1824, d. Weimar 1897) was the wife of Grand-Duke Charles Alexander (1818–1901). The last will and testament of Goethe's grandson, Walther von Goethe (d. 1885), bequeathed the Goethean Family Archive to her. She founded the Goethe Archive (subsequently the Goethe-Schiller Archive).

96. Bernhard Ludwig Suphan (b. Nordhausen 1845, d. Weimar 1911), literary historian. From 1887 until his death he was director of the Goethe-Schiller Archive. At the end of her volume *Rudolf Steiner in Weimar*, Dornach 1988, Jutta Hecker describes Suphan's tragic death as follows: 'He tied a noose, he piled up the volumes of his famous Herder edition and then, standing on top of them, kicked them resolutely away with his feet.'

97. The Goethe-Schiller Archive was initially housed within the ducal residence; in 1896 it moved across the river Ilm to the building erected by Sophie of Saxe-Weimar which to this day still serves as the Goethe Archive.

98. Richard Strauss (b. Munich 1864, d. Garmisch 1949), composer. From 1889 to 1894 he shared the post of court conductor at Weimar with Eduard Lassen.

99. *The Philosophy of Freedom, the Basis for a Modern World Conception*, Rudolf Steiner Press, London 1964 (GA 4).

100. *Truth and Knowledge.* See Note 85 on Rudolf Steiner's doctoral thesis.

101. The lecture in Vienna took place on 27 November 1891 before the Goethe Society. The subject was 'The Enigma of Goethe's Mysterious Tale in the "Conversations of German Émigrés"'. No record was made; however there is a report, possibly by K.J. Schröer, which was published in the 'Chronicles of the Vienna Goethe Society' 1891, Vol. V, Year 6, No. 12, p. 44. Reprinted in *Beiträge zur Rudolf Steiner Gesamtausgabe, Booklet 99/100.* See also Notes 126 and 127.

102. The second lecture, given before the Science Club in Vienna on 20 February 1893, entitled 'A Uniform View of Nature and the Limits of Knowledge', was printed in the 'Monatsblätter' of the Science Club, Vienna 1893, Year XIV, No. 10. See *Methodische Grundlagen der Anthroposophie* (GA 30).

103. This is evidently erroneous. Rudolf Steiner had a negative attitude toward Kant's philosophy, not Haeckel. Haeckel is mentioned only at the beginning of the talk: 'Ernst Haeckel, whom I, too, consider to be the greatest German natural scientist of the present day, wrote ...' This is followed by a quotation from Haeckel's book *History of Creation*. In *Methodische Grundlagen der Anthroposophie* (GA 30). See also Rudolf Steiner, 'Haeckel und seine Gegner' (1899) in the same volume (GA 30) of the collected works.

104. Annie Besant (b. London 1847, d. Adyar near Madras 1933). After a period of marked freedom of thought and social activity, she became a member of the Theosophical Society and a personal pupil of Blavatsky after reading her *Secret Doctrine*. She succeeded Blavatsky as leader of the Esoteric

School after her death; and after the death of Olcott, the Founding President, she also became President of the T.S. At the 1912 general meeting of the Theosophical Society in Adyar, Annie Besant stated the following about Rudolf Steiner: 'The German General-Secretary, educated by the Jesuits, has not been able to shake himself sufficiently clear of that fatal influence to allow freedom of opinion within his Section.' See *The Theosophist*, London February 1913.

105. In 1912 the Jesuit Otto Zimmermann had described Rudolf Steiner in *Stimmen aus Maria-Laach* (Freiburg im Breisgau 1912, Booklet 6) as '(reportedly) an apostate priest'. (In a review of *Manuale di Teosophia. Parte seconda: Teosophia e cristianesimo*, 2nd edition, Rome 1911 by Giovanni Busnelli, the author is quoted as saying 'formerly a Catholic priest'.

106. Rudolf Steiner, *Christianity as Mystical Fact*, Rudolf Steiner Press, London 1972 (GA 8). In Italian translation: Rodolfo Steiner, *Il Cristianesimo quale fatto mistico*, translated by Vittoria Wollisch with an introduction by E. Schuré, Palermo 1909.

107. Annie Besant, *Esoteric Christianity or The Lesser Mysteries*, Theosophical Publishing Society, London & Benares 1901. In Italian: Annie Besant, *Il Cristianesimo esoterico, o i misteri minori*, Rome 1903.

108. In the official Adyar bulletin in January 1913.

109. This is presumably a reference to the lecture to members at Graz on 22 January 1913. No records exist of any of the eight lectures given at Graz between 8 November 1907 and 22 January 1913.

110. See Note 73.

111. See Note 74.

112. Compelled, presumably, by Rudolf Steiner's question as to Annie Besant's 'sources' for her claims and by his energetic protest, Annie Besant soon named them in *The Theosophist*, London 1913 (April). See Eugène Lévy, *Mrs Annie Besant*

und die Krisis in der Theosophischen Gesellschaft, Berlin 1913,
p. 23. Those she named were: Dr Franz Hartmann, Paul
Zillmann and Dr Ferdinand Maack. As early on as 1909
Hartmann had mentioned the presumption about Rudolf
Steiner's 'Jesuitism'—and earlier on also that of Mrs
Besant—which she herself reported to Rudolf Steiner as an
absurdity (see Lévy, pp. 23f). In 1912 Zillmann, editor of
Neue Metaphysische Rundschau (Vol. XIX, pamphlet 5), had,
in his article 'Die Jesuiten und der Okkultismus', discussed
Rudolf Steiner's Jesuitical origins, referring to Otto Zimmermann and Ferdinand Maack, *Zweimal gestorben!*, Leipzig
1912. Maack also referred to Zimmermann and, based on his
statement about the 'apostate priest', declared Rudolf
Steiner's Jesuitical origins as 'proven'. In 1918 Otto Zimmermann S.J. himself showed the absurdity both of Besant's
remark about 'a pupil of Jesuits' and that of Busnelli S.J.
about the 'apostate priest' by adding the admittedly rather
superficial phrase 'which it has not been possible to prove'.
See *Stimmen der Zeit,* Freiburg im Breisgau 1918, Volume 95,
Year 48, Pamphlet 10, July, p. 331.

113. See Note 1.
114. See Note 4.
115. See Note 8.
116. See Note 9.
117. See Note 7.
118. See the description in the Berlin lecture of 4 February 1913
and also Note 12.
119. See Note 10.
120. See Note 18.
121. See Notes 13 and 14.
122. See Note 15.
123. See the various critiques contained in *Beiträge zur Rudolf
Steiner Gesamtausgabe, Booklet 85/86,* Dornach 1984, p. 41
and *Booklet 91,* Dornach 1986. Critiques and letters by the

literary historian Max Koch (1855–1931), Professor at Breslau, are reproduced in *Booklet 95/96*, Dornach 1987.

124. This is described by Rudolf Steiner at length in *The Course of My Life*, Chapter VI (GA 28). See also *Beiträge zur Rudolf Steiner Gesamtausgabe, Booklet 112/113*, edited by Walter Kugler, 'Rudolf Steiner als Hauslehrer und Erzieher, Wien 1884–1890'.

125. Testimonial regarding Rudolf Steiner's work as a tutor, presented by Ladislaus Specht on 8 January 1891, in *Rudolf Steiners Dissertation. Mit textkritischen Anmerkungen, Rezensionen und zahlreichen unveröffentlichten Briefen und Dokumenten zum Lebensgang Rudolf Steiners*, ed. David Hoffmann, Walter Kugler and Ulla Trapp in the series *Rudolf Steiner Studien*, Vol. I, Dornach 1991.

126. The handwriting is illegible here. The full title of the lecture was 'The Enigma of Goethe's Mysterious Tale in the "Conversations of German émigrés" '. See Note 101 and Note 127.

127. Newspaper critiques of the Vienna lecture and the two given at Weimar have been republished in *Beiträge zur Rudolf Steiner Gesamtausgabe, Booklet 99/100*. It was not yet customary for Rudolf Steiner's lectures to be recorded in shorthand, so there are no extant copies.

128. See Schuré's introduction to his translation into French of Rudolf Steiner's *Christianity as Mystical Fact*, in *Beiträge zur Rudolf Steiner Gesamtausgabe, Booklet 42*; also excerpts in Rudolf Steiner/Marie Steiner-von Sivers *Briefwechsel und Dokumente 1901–1925* p. 28; see also the Dornach lecture of 14 June 1923 in *The Anthroposophic Movement*, Rudolf Steiner Press, Bristol 1993 (GA 258); also Hella Wiesberger, 'Der biographische Entstehungsmoment der Zeiterkenntnis' and 'Die Zeiterkenntnis als "Grund-Nerv" des anthroposophischen Forschungsanfanges' in *Beiträge zur Rudolf Steiner Gesamtausgabe, Booklet 49/50*, pp. 15–28.

129. Nothing is known about this.

130. Felix Koguzki (b. Vienna 1833, d. Trumau 1909). See the autobiographical lecture given on 4 February 1913 (in the present volume) and also *The Course of My Life* (GA 28), Chapter III as well as Emil Bock, *The Life and Times of Rudolf Steiner, Vol. 1: People and Places*, Floris Books, Edinburgh 2008. See also Note 45.

131. See Note 44.

132. See Rudolf Steiner's biography of Ludwig Uhland (b. Tübingen 1787, d. Tübingen 1862), section 'Politik und Forschung. Universitätsprofessor' in Rudolf Steiner *Biographien und biographische Skizzen 1894–1905* (GA 33).

133. See Note 65.

134. See Note 75.

135. See Note 76.

136. See Note 79.

137. This is evidently a mistake. Rudolf Steiner's work as an educator and private tutor lasted for six years. See Note 72.

138. See Note 96.

139. This 'Nietzsche episode' is exhaustively documented in 'Rudolf Steiner und das Nietzsche-Archiv' in *Briefe und Dokumente 1894–1900*, ed. David Marc Hoffmann, Dornach 1993, Vol. VI in the series *Rudolf Steiner Studien* published by Rudolf Steiner Verlag.

140. Tönnies, Ferdinand, 'Ethische Cultur und ihr Geleite, I. Nietzsche-Narren, II. Wölfe in Fuchspelzen.' (two church magazines), Berlin 1893. See also Rudolf Steiner, 'Goethe-Studien. Moral und Christentum', an essay in the *Magazin für Literatur*, Year 69, August 1900, in *Methodische Grundlagen der Anthroposophie. Gesammelte Aufsätze 1884–1901* (GA 30).

141. See more in *Zur Geschichte und aus den Inhalten der ersten Abteilung der Esoterischen Schule 1904–1914* (GA 264). *From the History and Contents of the First Section of the Esoteric School 1904–1914*, Anthroposophic Press, Hudson 1998.

142. Marie von Sivers (b. Włocławek, Poland 1867, d. Beatenberg, Switzerland 1948) was Rudolf Steiner's closest colleague from 1902 onwards. They married in 1914. She had previously qualified as a performer in the Art of Recitation at the Paris Conservatory and in Drama in St Petersburg. She translated several works by Edouard Schuré into German. See *Marie Steiner-von Sivers, ein Leben für die Anthroposophie. Eine biographische Dokumentation*, ed. Hella Wiesberger, *Rudolf Steiner Studien*, Vol. 1, Dornach 1989.

143. See Rudolf Steiner, 'Die chymische Hochzeit des Christian Rosenkreutz' in *Philosophie und Anthroposophie 1904–1923* (GA 35). See also *Die chymische Hochzeit des Christian Rosenkreutz anno 1459*, translated into modern High German by Walter Weber, Stuttgart 1957 and Basel 1978. Also *Esoteric Christianity and the Mission of Christian Rosenkreutz*, Rudolf Steiner Press, London 1984 (GA 130).

144. See Rudolf Steiner, *Mysticism at the Dawn of the Modern Age*, Steinerbooks, 1980 (GA 7). See also the esoteric lesson given in Basel on 23 November 1907 in *Aus den Inhalten der Esoterischen Stunde* (GA 266/1), pp. 273ff. *Esoteric Lessons 1904–1909*, SteinerBooks, Great Barrington MA 2007. Also *Zur Geschichte und aus den Inhalten der ersten Abteilung der Esoterischen Schule 1904–1914* (GA 264) p. 230. For English see note 141. See also Wilhelm Rath, *The Friend of God from the High Lands*, Hawthorn Press, Stroud 1991.

145. See the lecture of 11 November 1904, Berlin, in *The Temple Legend*, Rudolf Steiner Press, London 1985 (GA 93).

146. Regarding the whole of the following section, see: *The Occult Movement in the Nineteenth Century and its Relation to Modern Culture*, Rudolf Steiner Press, London 1973 (GA 254); the lecture of 11 April 1912 in Helsingfors [Helsinki] in *Der Zusammenhang mit der elementarischen Welt* (GA 158): *Spiritual Beings in the Heavenly Bodies and the Kingdoms of Nature*, Anthroposophic Press, Hudson 1992; and also *Die Geschichte*

und die Bedingungen der anthroposophischen Bewegung im Verhältnis zur Anthroposophischen Gesellschaft (GA 258): *The Anthroposophic Movement*, op. cit.

147. The actual title was *Friedrich Nietzsche, Fighter for Freedom*, Rudolf Steiner Publications, New Jersey 1960 (GA 5). Steiner had published *Haeckel und seine Gegner* [Haeckel and his opponents] in 1900.

148. This appeared in 1904–05 as a sequence of essays in the journal *Lucifer-Gnosis*; first published as a book in 1909.

149. According to research by Carlo Septimus Picht during the 1920s, the 'written description' referred to comprises the early essays composed by Rudolf Steiner in 1882 or 1883 on 'Goethe und Shakespeare, eine Parallele' and on 'Lessing'. They had been published at Troppau during years II and III of the journal *Freie Schlesische Presse*. Originals of these essays have so far not been found and there are no known copies. See Note 67.

150. From 'How the Spiritual World Interpenetrates the Physical', Philosophical-Anthroposophical Publishing Company, Dornach 1927 (in GA 261).